ADVANCE PRAISE FOR

*Find a Real Friend in Jesus*

"*Find a Real Friend in Jesus* is a beautiful reminder of how much God truly loves us. Gary Zimak has written an inspired, practical guide for growing closer to Christ every day.... As you turn each page, you can almost feel Jesus wrap his arms of loving mercy and compassion around you. If you are seeking deeper intimacy and union with Christ in a simple yet powerful way, *Find a Real Friend in Jesus* will be your 'go to' resource."

Deacon Harold Burke-Sivers
author, *Behold the Man: A Catholic Vision of Male Spirituality*

"Friendship with Jesus is the key to keeping faith. It's the key to understanding theology. It's the key to evangelization. We tend to make things more complicated than they need to be. We need Gary Zimak to bring us back to divine simplicity."

Mike Aquilina
author, *Ministers and Martyrs:
The Ultimate Catholic Guide to the Apostolic Age*

"In this delightful book, Gary Zimak takes a subject that often feels amorphous and overwhelming and makes it clear and simple. It's a great resource for people who want a deeper relationship with God, but find that they have limited bandwidth for reading at the end of the day."

Jennifer Fulwiler
author, *Something Other Than God*
host, "The Jennifer Fulwiler Show"

"Zimak has a heart for calling everyone to experience a close, loving relationship with Jesus Christ. His prayerful love for Christ and personal experiences produce insights to which nearly every reader can relate about sacred Scripture, the power of the sacraments, the tenderness of the Blessed Virgin Mary, and the Church as a community of believers and source of wisdom. Post-modern, disgruntled Christians will benefit much from Zimak's book, especially those who are ready to return to their 'first love' of Christ in a joyful depth."

Fr. Mitch Pacwa, SJ
author and EWTN host

"Gary is a man on fire for Christ. He knows the transcendent joy that comes from saying yes to God. If you read this practical guide, he will help you say yes to the joy and peace of a living relationship with God. So pick up a copy, and discover for yourself the love your soul is longing for."

Dan Burke
president of the Avila Institute for Spiritual Formation
executive director, EWTN's *National Catholic Register*

❖ ❖ ❖

# find a
# real friend
# in Jesus

❖ ❖ ❖

## TEN AMAZINGLY EASY STEPS

❖ ❖ ❖

Gary Zimak

servant
AN IMPRINT OF
FRANCISCAN MEDIA
Cincinnati, Ohio

Scripture passages have been taken from the *Revised Standard Version*, Catholic edition. Copyright 1946, 1952, 1971 by the Division of Christian Education of the National Council of Churches of Christ in the USA. Used by permission. All rights reserved.

Quotes are taken from the English translation of the *Catechism of the Catholic Church* for the United States of America (indicated as CCC), 2nd ed. Copyright 1997 by United States Catholic Conference—Libreria Editrice Vaticana.

Cover design by LUCAS Art & Design
Cover image © Masterfile
Book design by Mark Sullivan

Library of Congress Control Number: 2015959786

ISBN 978-1-63253-022-6
Copyright ©2016 Gary Zimak. All rights reserved.

Published by Servant,
an imprint of Franciscan Media
28 W. Liberty St.
Cincinnati, OH 45202
www.FranciscanMedia.org

*To my wife, Eileen:*

Every day, you teach me the meaning of unconditional love. Thank you for being my best friend and for your constant support of my work. I love you!

*To my daughters, Elizabeth and Mary:*

You are proof that miracles still happen. Thank you for being such wonderful young ladies. The world is a better place because of you. I love you both!

*To my Blessed Mother:*

Thank you, Mary, for helping me to follow Jesus. I love you very much, and I can't wait to see where we go next!

*To Jesus:*

I am so grateful to be your friend, Lord. Please bless all who read this book. Thank you for being so patient with me. I love you!

*To my friends at Servant Books:*

Thank you for believing in me. You are a great blessing, and I am grateful for the chance to write about my friend Jesus.

*To all who have prayed for this project:*

This book would not have been possible without your prayers. You got me through some very difficult and dry spells. I am extremely grateful. May the Lord bless you abundantly!

# contents

Imagine for a minute that a complete stranger came up to you and asked a simple question: "Do you know Jesus?"

How would you answer? Assuming you would say yes, let's pause and consider some potential follow-up questions from our hypothetical stranger:

"What can you tell me about him?"

"What are his likes and dislikes?"

"Do you speak with him frequently?"

"How often do you visit him?"

"How can I get to know him?"

Interesting questions, aren't they? If they make you feel uncomfortable, don't panic. In all honesty, these questions will probably make many people a little uneasy. Trying to answer them usually makes us realize that our relationship with Jesus isn't what it should be. And that realization is not a bad thing at all. It isn't until we know that there is a problem with our relationship that we can take steps to correct it.

As someone who was baptized into the Catholic faith and went to Mass every Sunday for all of my life, I can assure you that not everyone who goes to church has a close, personal relationship with Jesus. Even though I received him every week in Holy Communion, I didn't know Jesus. And it wasn't his fault at all. It was mine!

For years the Lord was right beside me, asking me to be his friend. Unfortunately, I was too busy to respond. The only time I ever spoke with him was when I needed something. In an emergency, I always seemed to remember Jesus. I knew where to find him when I was in trouble, but I would forget about him as soon as he answered my prayer.

This reminds me of an old joke: A man was late for a job interview, and he was frantically searching for a parking spot. He drove up and down the aisles of the parking structure, and there was not a spot in sight. Finally, in an act of desperation, he cried out to the Lord, "Lord, if you help me find a parking spot, I promise to turn my life around. I'll pray every day and give up cheating on my taxes and watching bad TV shows." Just as he finished his prayer, the man discovered a vacant parking spot. "Never mind, Lord," he exclaimed, "I found one!"

Jesus loves us unconditionally, and he absolutely wants us to turn to him when we're in trouble. A health scare in 2004 got my attention and made me seriously pursue a close relationship with the Lord. But Jesus also wants us to turn to him when we're not in trouble. He is much more than someone who bails us out when we need something.

Even though Jesus and I speak every day now, I'm not content. In fact, I will spend the rest of my life trying to grow closer to him. Just as I desire to do with my wife, I want to get to know and love Jesus more each day.

Now, you may be reading this and thinking that you don't know where to start with getting to know Jesus personally. The good news is that you have already started by picking up this book. By the time you finish reading it, you will have ten *amazingly* easy steps that will help draw you closer to the Lord. While these steps require some work on your part, they are simple enough that anyone can put them into practice.

It's also important to remember that you're not the only one working on your relationship with Jesus. This is a relationship that Jesus wants even more than you do! Once you start speaking to him more and spending time in his presence, he will share more of himself with you. In other words, he'll do some of the work. With both of you working on the relationship, you will grow closer to one another. You'll also receive help from God the Father, the Holy Spirit, Mary, and the Church!

As you move through the following chapters, you'll learn how much Jesus loves you and how much he wants to be your friend. Even if every other person in the world responds to his offer of friendship, he will have a sense of emptiness until you respond. We'll open the Bible and look at how lives were changed forever because of encounters with Jesus. Then we'll explore concrete steps that you can take to grow closer to the Lord. These techniques will bear fruit in your life.

No matter where you are in your spiritual journey, this book is designed for you. If you've never spoken to Jesus, you'll learn how to get started. If you speak to him infrequently, you'll discover ways to speak to him more often. Even if you already have a close personal relationship with the Lord, you won't be excluded, as we'll discuss ways to keep your relationship fresh.

In the book of Revelation, Jesus makes an offer to each of us: "Behold, I stand at the door and knock; if any one hears my voice and opens the door, I will come in to him and eat with him, and he with me" (Revelation 3:20). His words serve as a reminder that he will not force himself into our lives. It is up to us to answer the door and invite him in. If we respond, he will enter more deeply into our lives. It's as simple as that.

You have already responded to the Lord's knocking by opening this book. As you sit before him, you face an important decision that only you can make. Are you ready to invite Jesus more deeply into your life?

## chapter one

## Good Relationships Don't Just Happen

⸙ ⸙ ⸙

I love those who love me,
and those who seek me diligently find me.
—Proverbs 8:17

Since this book is all about having a personal relationship with Jesus, it's important for us to understand some basic concepts about relationships. Although there are differences in how we relate to the Lord as opposed to another human, many of the same principles apply. Knowing what it takes to establish and maintain a good relationship with another person will help us enter into a deeper relationship with Christ.

While most people understand the concept of a personal relationship, it's sometimes not the easiest thing to describe. Basically, it can be defined as two people connecting with one another in some way. In order for a personal relationship to exist, there must be some contact between the individuals.

When I was young, I knew many facts about baseball players and rock stars. I could tell you how old they were, where they were born, and maybe even their favorite foods. Knowing about these individuals, however, didn't mean that I knew them personally. It was not possible for me to have a personal relationship with any of them. On the other hand, I had several friends whom I did know personally and with whom it was possible to enter into a relationship.

The first rule of relationships is that the two people must know each other. Secondly, there must be some degree of communication between the individuals. Is that all it takes? Well, yes and no. Not all relationships are created equal. There is a big difference between a relationship and a close (or intimate) personal relationship.

Let's look at some of the things that will help a relationship flourish. We'll also briefly explore how each of these principles will help in our quest to grow closer to the Lord.

### Self-Sacrifice

In order for a relationship to be successful, I must learn to put the needs of the other person before my own. If both individuals put this into practice, everyone gets taken care of, and the relationship will be a good one. Self-sacrifice is a necessary component of any loving relationship.

If I am to enter into a close relationship with the Lord, I should also be willing to put him first. Accepting suffering willingly, helping the poor, and praying even when I don't feel like it are some ways to put this into practice. Incidentally, there is no need to worry about the Lord's holding up his end of the bargain. He loves us unconditionally and always puts us first.

### Commitment

Good relationships don't just happen; they require work. And both parties must be willing to work. My wife and I have the grace that flows from the sacrament of marriage, but we still have to work at our relationship. We work at it every day, whether we feel like it or not. We are committed to our union and are willing to do whatever is necessary to allow it to grow.

Growing closer to the Lord also requires work; it doesn't just happen. We can rest assured that God will do his part. It's up to us to commit to the relationship for the long haul. If we hang in there and are willing to do whatever it takes, our relationship with God will grow.

### HONESTY

Honesty is an important part of any close relationship. Not only must deception be avoided at all cost, but both parties must be willing to share their true feelings. This act of mutual openness draws individuals together and allows them to act as one.

When dealing with the Lord, honesty still applies. Even though he knows when we're being dishonest and there really is no way we can deceive him, we must be willing to express our true feelings to him. As scary as it sounds, this even means expressing our lack of trust in him and asking for help. That total openness will help us grow closer to him.

### TIME TOGETHER

While time together seems obvious as a prerequisite for a good relationship, its importance sometimes gets overlooked. The more time individuals in a relationship spend together, the closer they will become. This principle not only applies to the initial stages of a relationship but is also true for the duration. In order to grow closer to another person, you must spend time together.

How much time? While I can't give you an exact number of minutes or hours, I can tell you that one hour a week is not enough. That won't work with a spouse or a good friend, and it won't work with God. Many people think that going to Mass each week is all they need to remain close to the Lord. But in order to have a close, personal relationship with Jesus, we must spend time with him every day. And that time is never wasted!

## ADMITTING MISTAKES

Let's face it, we all make mistakes. Learning to admit when you have made a mistake is crucial to the success of a relationship. What is even more important is the ability to apologize when you're wrong. The words "I'm sorry" are powerful; they need to be a regular part of our vocabulary.

In our relationship with the Lord, we're going to be the one making the mistakes. When we goof up (and it will happen), we need to admit that we are wrong, express our sorrow (the sacrament of reconciliation is perfect for that), and ask for the grace to do better next time. God doesn't expect us to be perfect. He does expect us, however, to admit when we're wrong and ask for his help along the way.

## KEEPING FEELINGS IN PERSPECTIVE

We are constantly bombarded with the message that love is a feeling. While it is true that we often feel affection toward those whom we love, we shouldn't let ourselves be ruled by our feelings. Love is a conscious decision. We can choose to love someone, even if we do not feel like it. Most parents don't relish waking up in the middle of the night to comfort a crying baby. Rather, they do it out of love.

No matter how much you love the Lord, there will be days when you don't feel like praying. If you want to have a close, personal relationship with him, you must commit to praying every day, whether you feel like it or not.

## APPRECIATION

It's nice to be appreciated, isn't it? While it shouldn't be the goal of doing good deeds for others, it certainly feels great to hear the words *Thank you*. Yet we often forget to express our appreciation for acts of kindness directed our way. We take people for granted. One of the best ways for a relationship to grow is to learn how to say thank you.

In Luke's Gospel, the evangelist tells of the encounter between Jesus and ten lepers (see Luke 17:11–19). After the miraculous healing, only one of them, a Samaritan, returned to thank the Lord. "Then said Jesus, 'Were not ten cleansed? Where are the nine? Was no one found to return and give praise to God except this foreigner?'" (Luke 17:17–18). If we expect to grow in our relationship with Christ, we need to imitate that Samaritan and offer thanks.

## EXPRESSIONS OF LOVE

I have been married for twenty years, and my wife and I have said "I love you" to one another at least once each day for all of those years. Even though I know that Eileen loves me, I never get tired of hearing those words. While it's certainly important to show loved ones that we care about them, it's also important to tell them.

In our relationship with the Lord, we sometimes think that it's not necessary to express our love for him. After all, he knows everything, so why bother? Even though he is all-knowing, he enjoys hearing the words "I love you." Getting into the habit of saying those words will draw you closer to him.

## ADMIRATION

My wife is a fantastic person. She has many great qualities—kindness, beauty, charm, sense of humor, a strong faith....

When I spend time thinking about her many wonderful traits, it makes me appreciate her more. It reminds me of why I fell in love with her in the first place.

It's a good idea to reflect regularly on the wonderful qualities of Our Lord—his great power, unconditional love, approachability, and so on. Let's not take the Lord of the universe, our Redeemer and Savior, for granted!

## A Sense of Humor

I'm not joking about this: Sometimes we take ourselves too seriously. We forget to laugh at some of the silly things that we do and say. Having a sense of humor is not only important in relationships, but it's very helpful in dealing with our daily challenges. I'm certainly not recommending that we laugh at inappropriate times, but sometimes a little laughter can be just what the doctor ordered.

Have you ever heard the expression, "If you want to make God laugh, tell him your plans"? That is a good one to remember when unexpected difficulties arise in our lives. Like the woman in Proverbs 31, let's learn to laugh at the times to come, knowing that we are in God's hands (see Proverbs 31:25).

Now that we have looked at some of the vital components in a healthy relationship, how do we apply them to our relationship with God? After all, we can't really see him, hear him, or be sure that he is listening to us. Is the Lord more than an imaginary friend?

In reality, God loves us and wants to have a close relationship with us. In fact, he loves us so much that he took an extraordinary step in order to make that possible: He became one of us. In the following chapter, we'll look at how "the Word became flesh and dwelt among us" (John 1:14).

DON'T FORGET...

1. In any relationship, we must be willing to put the needs of the other individual before our own.

2. Love isn't a feeling; it is a conscious decision.

3. Spending time with one another is an essential part of a healthy relationship.

4. Remember to say, "Thank you," "I'm sorry," and, "I love you."

5. It is totally possible to have a close, personal relationship with the Lord, provided we're willing to work at it.

JESUS SAYS...

"Greater love has no man than this, that a man lay down his life for his friends." (John 15:13) chapter two

# How Much Does God Love You?

✳ ✳ ✳

I have loved you with an everlasting love;
therefore I have continued my faithfulness to you.
—JEREMIAH 31:3

Each week on the popular television series *Undercover Boss*, viewers tune in to see top executives go "undercover" in their own companies. It is fascinating to see disguised CEOs washing dishes, scrubbing floors, and waiting on customers. At the end of their assignments, corporate officers have a much better idea of the daily struggles of their employees. An undercover experience usually results in a series of charitable steps performed by the executive, designed to relieve the burdens of employees.

While that aspect of the show is very heartwarming, it's also interesting to watch the reactions of the workers once the secret is revealed. In almost every episode, at least one employee expresses gratitude that the boss would care enough to take this extraordinary step. The employee recognizes the boss's humility and concern for the lives of others.

As commendable as it is that these top-level executives want to become personally involved in the lives of their employees, it's also a logical move on their part. It makes good business sense. Generally speaking, happy employees are going to be more productive than unhappy employees.

In addition, workers are typically not responsible for difficult working conditions. Many of the challenges they encounter in their work environments are caused by poor management decisions or procedures. In a certain sense, the executives have responsibility for any mess that they have created. One could even argue that they owe it to the employees to make positive changes.

So when these executives become personally involved in the lives of their employees, there is something in it for them. Their actions would be even more impressive if they performed them purely out of love. If we go back to the beginning of time, we see an example of that kind of generosity. Without a doubt, it's something that is more magnanimous than anything you will ever see on *Undercover Boss*. It's the prime example of pure, unconditional love.

THE FATHER'S PLAN

Although he had absolutely nothing to gain from it, God wanted to share his very life with man. As a result, he began the process of creation. In the first two chapters of the book of Genesis, we see how the Lord created the heavens and the earth from nothing. He then populated the earth with numerous creatures. God's act of generosity culminated with the creation of man.

Why did God do this? He did it solely out of love. According to the *Catechism of the Catholic Church*, "God, infinitely perfect and blessed in himself, in a plan of sheer goodness freely created man to make him share in his own blessed life. For this reason, at every time and in every place, God draws close to man" (CCC 1).

God is infinitely perfect and doesn't need anything. It wasn't loneliness that prompted him to create man. He did it because he wanted to share his life with us, a life that consists of perfect happiness. That's how loving he is! In fact, "God is love" (1 John 4:8).

Man was created in God's own image and likeness and was invited to enter into a personal relationship with him. Think about that for a minute. It is an astonishing concept. It's great that man was created and placed in Paradise, but it's even better that he was invited to know and love his Creator personally.

God wants to have a relationship with us. He desires it simply out of love. There is no ulterior motive on his part. And the best news of all is that nothing, not even sin or lack of interest on our part, can ever change his desire to have an intimate relationship with us. God's love for us is totally unconditional. He loves *you* just for being *you*!

I recommend that you read through Genesis 1 and 2; it's such a great story. Let's take a look at one verse that reflects what happened in that initial process of creation: "And God saw everything that he had made, and behold, it was very good" (Genesis 1:31).

Note that God saw creation not just as good but as very good. His plan was that man would have everything he needed and live in a loving relationship with his Creator. What a great and generous plan it was! Try to imagine a world where there are no problems or suffering, a world where we would love God (and others) unconditionally. It would be total happiness, all the time.

Adam and Eve were created out of love, had a perfect relationship with the Lord, and had everything they needed.

Unfortunately, they let their own desires get in the way. Their selfishness caused a rift between God and man. Their disobedience brought sin and death into the world. Paradise was shattered.

Although Adam and Eve's actions caused major damage, it was not irreparable damage. Because he is all-loving, God would not give up on the relationship with man.

> He calls man to seek him, to know him, to love him with all his strength. He calls together all men, scattered and divided by sin, into the unity of his family, the Church. To accomplish this, when the fullness of time had come, God sent his Son as Redeemer and Savior. In his Son and through him, he invites men to become, in the Holy Spirit, his adopted children and thus heirs of his blessed life. (CCC 1)

As soon as Adam and Eve sinned, God promised to send a Savior (see Genesis 3:15) to repair the damage caused by their disobedience. Even though the Lord was in no way responsible for their sins, he desired to restore the relationship with his creatures. And the damage was so great that it would require an unimaginable "fix." That "fix" would eventually result in God's becoming man!

As he typically does, God proceeded according to his own schedule. Instead of having the Savior appear immediately, the process took thousands of years to unfold. But the wheels were set in motion, and the story of salvation history began to unfold.

As we discussed in the previous chapter, it is impossible for a relationship to develop between parties who do not know one another. While God certainly knew man, fallen man didn't know

God. There was a great deal to be learned about the Creator. God would gradually reveal himself to man.

> God, who "dwells in unapproachable light," wants to communicate his own divine life to the men he freely created, in order to adopt them as his sons in his only-begotten Son [see 1 Timothy 6:16; Ephesians 1:4–5]. By revealing himself God wishes to make them capable of responding to him, and of knowing him, and of loving him far beyond their own natural capacity.
>
> The divine plan of Revelation is realized simultaneously "by deeds and words which are intrinsically bound up with each other" and shed light on each other. It involves a specific divine pedagogy: God communicates himself to man gradually. He prepares him to welcome by stages the supernatural Revelation that is to culminate in the person and mission of the incarnate Word, Jesus Christ. (CCC 52–53, quoting *Dei Verbum*, 2)

Throughout the Old Testament, we see numerous accounts of God's revelation to man. The Lord communicated with Abraham, Moses, and many prophets. He revealed himself in his marvelous works of redemption—saving Noah and his family from the Flood, bringing Israel through the Red Sea, establishing his kingdom under David. As a result, his creatures began to know the Creator. Despite these eye-opening revelations, however, there was still much to be learned about God. He was saving the best for last.

When the time was right, God revealed himself in the fullest way possible: "In many and various ways God spoke of old to our fathers by the prophets; but in these last days he has spoken to us by a Son, whom he appointed the heir of all things, through whom also he created the ages" (Hebrews 1:1–2).

In a far superior way to what can be seen each week on *Undercover Boss*, "the Word became flesh and dwelt among us, full of grace and truth" (John 1:14). While most of us recognize the fact that he did this to make reparation for the sins of mankind, there is another all-encompassing summary of his selfless act: "The Word became flesh *so that thus we might know God's love*" (CCC 458).

IT'S ALL ABOUT LOVE

Once again, we turn to that familiar theme: God loves us so much that he was not willing to let us live apart from him. God was not about to abandon us. He still desired to have a personal relationship with his creatures, even though it took his Son to become man, suffer, and die.

> In this the love of God was made manifest among us, that God sent his only-begotten Son into the world, so that we might live through him. In this is love, not that we loved God but that he loved us and sent his Son to be the expiation for our sins. (1 John 4:9–10)

Sometimes this kind of love sounds too good to be true. No matter how hard we try, it's difficult to wrap our brains around the idea of unconditional love. It's even more challenging to put it into practice in our lives. Even if we try to love others unconditionally, we often fail. People don't live up to our expectations. We can forgive once or twice, but we usually have our limit. Our fallen human nature makes it difficult to love those we find annoying, not to mention our enemies.

Fortunately, God doesn't love in a human way. Instead he loves in a divine way. There is nothing we can ever do to make God not love us. Through Jesus, we are able to share in that love to the fullest extent possible. The Son of God not only makes it possible for us to know God, but he makes it possible for us to love him in an intimate way. "No one has ever seen God; the only-begotten Son, who is in the bosom of the Father, he has made him known" (John 1:18).

When we encounter Jesus, we encounter the Father. Jesus "is the Father's one, perfect, and unsurpassable Word. In him he has said everything" (CCC 65). By entering into a relationship with Jesus, we also enter into a relationship with our heavenly Father. This relationship will not only enable us to know the Father but also transform our earthly life. Furthermore, through Jesus, it will be possible for us to live forever in heaven. At the heart of this relationship is pure, unconditional love.

How can we be sure?

> While we were yet helpless, at the right time Christ died for the ungodly. Why, one will hardly die for a righteous man—though perhaps for a good man one will dare even to die. But God shows his love for us in that while we were yet sinners Christ died for us. (Romans 5:6–8)

That is what unconditional love looks like.

Jesus is a real person who loves you with an everlasting love. He wants to be your friend. If you choose to accept his offer, you will enter into the best relationship of your life.

> For God so loved the world that he gave his only-begotten Son, that whoever believes in him should not perish but have eternal life. (John 3:16)

Don't Forget...

1. Although he had nothing to gain from it, God wanted to share his very life with man.

2. As soon as Adam and Eve sinned, God promised that a Savior would be sent (see Genesis 3:15) to repair the damage caused by their disobedience.

3. The Father's love can be expressed in one word: *Jesus.*

4. No one comes to the Father except through Christ.

5. In Jesus, the Father's revelation to man is complete.

Jesus Says...

"He who has seen me has seen the Father." (John 14:9)

## chapter three

## Your *Best* Best Friend

\* \* \*

For we have not a high priest who is unable to sympathize with
our weaknesses, but one who in every respect has been tempted
as we are, yet without sinning.

—HEBREWS 4:15

Friendship is a great thing. Over the course of my life, I've
been blessed with many friends. The vast majority have
been just that—friends. On the other hand, a few select individuals stand out above the rest. They would fall into the category
of best friends. These friends are the ones who have been there
for me, in good times and bad. I have found even the baddest of
bad days bearable when I have a best friend in my life.

Through the years, I've had many best friends. The names
were different in grade school, high school, college, and post-
college, but someone always filled that role in my life. All of
these best friends had some things in common:

*Reliability:* Best friends are always there when you need them.
It doesn't matter whether it's day or night, convenient or incon-
venient. They are there for you.

*Interest:* A best friend will always be interested in your life,
even in the minute details.

*No Conditions:* Nothing you say or do will cause best friends to withdraw their friendship.

*Selflessness:* Best friends always put your happiness before their own. Even when helping you out is uncomfortable or costly, they will strive to be there for you.

At this point in time, I am happily married to my best friend. It would be no exaggeration to say that Eileen has far exceeded my expectations for a best friend. I am truly blessed to have her in my life.

However, with all due respect to Eileen and to best friends everywhere, there is someone who gives a whole new meaning to the term "best friend." A friendship with this individual is so far superior to any relationship you've ever experienced that it borders on incomprehensible. Given this, one might think that it's not easy to become friends with such a person. After all, why would such a desirable individual want to be friends with me?

Fortunately, it is surprisingly easy to enter into a friendship with this amazing individual. He wants to be your best friend. You may have already guessed, but his name is Jesus Christ.

WHAT A FRIEND WE HAVE IN JESUS!

Before we look at some of the compelling reasons for becoming friends with Christ, let's look at who this guy is. Even though Jesus is fully God, he is also fully human. That means that, like us, the Second Person of the Trinity knows what it's like to be hungry, thirsty, tired, sad, and happy. He freely chose to experience the human emotions and sensations that we deal with on a daily basis. You and I don't have a choice, but the Word of God did. I find that astounding.

> Have this mind among yourselves, which was in Christ
> Jesus, who, though he was in the form of God, did not
> count equality with God a thing to be grasped, but emptied
> himself, taking the form of a servant, being born in the
> likeness of men. (Philippians 2:5–7)

How generous was the Lord's gesture?

Imagine for a moment that it's the middle of winter, and the temperatures are in the single digits. You are warm inside your cozy home and thankful for the many blessings in your life. You turn on the news, and suddenly your mood changes. You see a story about the homeless in your city. Moved with compassion, you make the decision that you want to help them in some way.

You decide to sell most of your possessions and use the money to clothe and feed the homeless in your area. But then you realize that you want to take it a step further. You want to become one with those whom you are helping. You want to suffer as they suffer and help them "from within." As a result, you make the radical decision to sell your home so that you can become homeless yourself.

Despite the bitterly cold temperature and the dangers of living on the street, you take a few belongings and a sleeping bag and head to the downtown area. There you will become one with the people you desire to help, even though it will cause you great discomfort and pain. The suffering for which you are heading is drowned out by the love you feel for those you want to help.

As selfless as this gesture would be, it's only a shadow of what Jesus was willing to endure for you. He voluntarily left the comfort of paradise to help those he loved. That's what I call a *best* best friend!

Lest there's any doubt in your mind about Jesus's qualifications to be your *best* best friend, let's examine those four character traits that we looked at earlier and see how he measures up.

Jesus promised to remain with us until the end of time (see Matthew 28:20). One can't get much more reliable than that.

Jesus cared enough to become man in order to save us from our sins and to leave us his real presence in the Eucharist. I think that proves that he has an interest in our lives.

What about unconditional love? Is there anything we could ever do to lose the friendship of Christ? Absolutely not. The fact that he instituted the sacrament of penance (with no limit on the number of times we can be forgiven) indicates that his friendship isn't conditional.

Finally, we could never come up with a more selfless act of friendship than Jesus's laying down his life for us.

I think it's safe to say that Jesus Christ has all of the qualities (and more) needed to qualify for *best* best friend status!

## JESUS WANTS YOU!

But should we become friends with Jesus? After all, can't we just do what he tells us and get to heaven anyway? Why is it so important to be friends with him? Does he really care that we become his friends? Couldn't we just stay away from sin and leave it at that? These are all very reasonable questions, ones that should be addressed.

Let's first look at the idea of following the Lord's commands. While it's not ordinarily the first thing that pops into our minds when we think of friendship with Jesus, it is a critical element of that friendship. Jesus made that clear when he said, "You are my friends if you do what I command you" (John 15:14). Does this imply that all I have to do to be friends with Jesus is do what he commands?

Not necessarily. While obedience to the commandments of Jesus can be a great expression of your love for him, you could be obeying for different reasons. You could be afraid of going to hell. You could be aiming for superiority over others or be looking for praise. God is looking for something more from us.

Jesus desires our love. In fact, he will be sad if we don't enter into a loving relationship with him. Yes, that's right: Rejecting his offer of friendship will make Jesus sad.

But with all of Jesus's other friends, does my friendship really matter that much to him? Absolutely! Although it may be hard to believe, the Lord loves you as if you're the only person in the world. He desperately wants to be friends with you.

OK, but what about that sadness thing? Will Jesus really be sad if I don't feel the need to be his friend?

A look at Jesus's time on earth reminds us that he experienced the same feelings that you and I deal with each day. The Bible tells us that he wept at the death of his friend Lazarus (see John 11:35), displayed compassion for the helpless crowds (see Matthew 9:36), had a troubled soul (see John 12:27), and experienced hunger (see Mark 11:12) and tiredness (see John 4:6). On the night before he died, Jesus's humanity was evident in a big way. Not only did he experience a feeling of dread, but he reached out to his closest friends for support:

> Then Jesus went with them to a place called Gethsemane, and he said to his disciples, "Sit here, while I go over there and pray." And taking with him Peter and the two sons of Zebedee, he began to be sorrowful and troubled. Then he

said to them, "My soul is very sorrowful, even to death; remain here, and watch with me." And going a little farther he fell on his face and prayed, "My Father, if it be possible, let this chalice pass from me; nevertheless, not as I will, but as you will." (Matthew 26:36–39)

This passage gives us a detailed glimpse into the humanity of Christ. He even asked his Father to let the chalice of suffering pass him by. His disappointment in finding his closest human friends asleep is obvious: "Are you still sleeping and taking your rest?" (Matthew 26:45). "Could you not watch one hour?" (Mark 14:37). These details should erase from our minds any thought that Jesus can't be sad. He knows what it's like to suffer, both mentally and physically.

One could argue, however, that this occurred two thousand years ago; things are different now. Isn't Jesus in heaven, where there is no sadness or pain? How is it possible for him to be sad? How can my refusal of friendship affect him in any way? It's a valid point and one that needs to be addressed.

## Solace for the Savior

While it is true that Jesus no longer suffers in the same way he did two thousand years ago, our rejection of his offer of friendship can still grieve him. Pope Pius XI sheds some light on the matter in his encyclical on the Sacred Heart of Jesus. He takes us back in time to the night of Jesus's suffering in the Garden of Gethsemane:

Now if, because of our sins also which were as yet in the future, but were foreseen, the soul of Christ became sorrowful unto death, it cannot be doubted that then, too, already He derived somewhat of solace from our reparation, which was likewise foreseen, when "there appeared to him an angel from heaven" (Luke 22:43), in order that His Heart, oppressed with weariness and anguish, might find consolation. And so even now, in a wondrous yet true manner, we can and ought to console that Most Sacred Heart which is continually wounded by the sins of thankless men, since—as we also read in the sacred liturgy—Christ Himself, by the mouth of the Psalmist complains that He is forsaken by His friends: "My Heart hath expected reproach and misery, and I looked for one that would grieve together with me, but there was none: and for one that would comfort me, and I found none" (Psalm 69:20).[1]

This is an amazing concept—one that blew me away when I first heard it. And now it's something that affects every day of my life. Let me explain.

We've already established the fact that Jesus suffered greatly in the garden, but the Holy Father takes it to the next level. Pope Pius XI tells us that one of the main reasons that Jesus suffered so greatly on the night before he died is our sins, past and future. On that night, Jesus was able to look into the future and see every single time that you and I would betray him by sinning. He also knew all of the times that we would ignore him and reject his offer of friendship. As moving and thought-provoking as this revelation is, however, the best is yet to come!

The Holy Father alludes to the fact that Jesus found solace and consolation in our future acts of reparation. Is that mind-boggling or what? Just think of the possibilities that this opens up! By accepting the Lord's offer of friendship and trying to grow closer to him, we are able to take away some of his suffering on that night in the garden. Even though Peter, James, and John fell asleep and left Jesus to suffer alone, we can comfort him. Not only will we benefit from being friends with Christ, but in a mysterious way, so will he.

As wonderful as this sounds, what happens if we reject his offer of friendship? That will mean one less act of consolation for Jesus in his hour of need. As incredulous as it may seem, our friendship does make a difference in the life of Jesus.

Jesus expressed his longing for our friendship in his words to St. Margaret Mary Alacoque:

> I feel this more than all that I suffered during my Passion. If only they would make Me some return for My love, I should think but little of all I have done for them and would wish, were it possible, to suffer still more. But the sole return they make for all My eagerness to do them good is to reject Me and treat Me with coldness.[2]

Are you ready to become close friends with Christ? We'll examine how to do this later in the book, but for now let's focus on saying yes to Jesus's invitation of friendship. I guarantee that your life will never be the same. You will have the *best* best friend you could ever imagine.

In the next chapter, we'll look at the lives of people who encountered Jesus. They were forever changed. You will be too!

Don't Forget...

1. Jesus desires to be close friends with each of us.
2. Our best friend is reliable, is interested in our life, loves us unconditionally, and is selfless.

3. Rejecting Christ's offer of friendship causes him to suffer.

4. Jesus suffered great agony as he faced the pain of the cross, but his love and surrender to the Father's will never wavered.

5. Every act of friendship directed toward Jesus today is mysteriously able to ease the agony he suffered two thousand years ago.

JESUS SAYS…

"No longer do I call you servants, for the servant does not know what his master is doing; but I have called you friends, for all that I have heard from my Father I have made known to you." (John 15:15)

## chapter four

## Close Encounters of the Divine Kind

*   *   *

And all the crowd sought to touch him, for power came forth
from him and healed them all.

—LUKE 6:19

An encounter with Jesus can be a life-changing experience. In his book *Life of Christ*, Archbishop Fulton Sheen
reflected on the fact that, after seeing the Messiah in person, the
wise men from the East went home "by another way" (Matthew
2:12). "No one who ever meets Christ with good will," wrote
Archbishop Sheen, "returns the same way as he came."[3]

In this chapter, we're going to open the Bible and look at
several encounters with Jesus. It is truly remarkable to see what
can happen to an individual who meets Christ. Even the briefest
of encounters can bear fruit a hundredfold. As you read through
the details of these meetings, try to imagine the impact of a
close, personal relationship with Jesus in your life.

SIMEON (LUKE 2:25–35)
A holy man who lived in Jerusalem, Simeon was informed by
the Holy Spirit that he would not see death before encountering
the Messiah. Inspired by that same Spirit, he came to the Temple
one day for a life-changing meeting. On that day, in obedience

to the Mosaic law, Mary and Joseph brought the infant Jesus to the Temple, to present him to the Lord and offer an appropriate sacrifice. Upon seeing the child, Simeon took him in his arms and blessed God:

> Lord, now let your servant depart in peace,
> according to your word;
> for my eyes have seen your salvation
> which you have prepared in the presence of all peoples,
> a light for revelation to the Gentiles,
> and for glory to your people Israel. (Luke 2:29–32)

Simeon felt that his life was complete. He had seen the Messiah. Since Jesus was still an infant, he didn't even speak to Simeon. The mere presence of the Lord was enough to profoundly affect the elderly man. Can you imagine having this kind of appreciation for the Lord's real presence every time you receive him in Holy Communion?

## THE APOSTLES

I could probably fill a book with an analysis of the relationships between Jesus and the apostles. Let's just look at a few examples. We'll examine their initial encounter with him and their final encounter with him, as he ascended into heaven.

What is it like to meet Jesus for the first time? Let's take a look at the calls of Simon, Andrew, James, and John:

> As he walked by the Sea of Galilee, he saw two brothers, Simon who is called Peter and Andrew his brother, casting a net into the sea; for they were fishermen. And he said to them, "Follow me, and I will make you fishers of men." Immediately they left their nets and followed him. And

going on from there he saw two other brothers, James the son of Zebedee and John his brother, in the boat with Zebedee their father, mending their nets, and he called them. Immediately they left the boat and their father, and followed him. (Matthew 4:18–22)

After being called by Jesus, all four men left their fishing jobs—immediately! Now, I invite you to carefully examine the Lord's words and put yourself in the shoes of the fishermen. What did Jesus say that would cause them to immediately abandon their livelihoods and follow him? Nothing, right? Just as we saw with Simeon, it wasn't Jesus's words that first moved the apostles; it was his very presence!

Scripture indicates that this initial zeal to follow the Lord sometimes flagged. (The apostles were very human.) They would argue over who was the greatest, set their sights on the highest honors, and fall asleep when Jesus most needed their support (see Mark 9:34; 10:35–37; 14:37–41). Even after the Resurrection, Peter was ready to return to his former occupation: "I am going fishing." And the others agreed: "We will go with you" (John 21:3).

Let's fast-forward to the final encounter of the apostles with Jesus. An ongoing personal relationship with him and the gift of the Holy Spirit had quite transformed them. After seeing Jesus crucified, being told that he would be ascending into heaven, and being instructed to carry on his work (see Matthew 28:19–20), the apostles, we might expect, were less than thrilled. But in an often overlooked detail provided by St. Luke, we once again see the power that comes from being close to the Lord:

> While he blessed them, he parted from them, and was carried up into heaven. And they worshipped him, and returned to Jerusalem with great joy, and were continually in the temple blessing God. (Luke 24:51–53)

"Great joy"? Jesus was leaving them to carry on the work that resulted in his being put to death, and they were joyful. Now, that's incredible!

### THE WOMAN AT THE WELL (JOHN 4:1–42)

On a journey from Judea to Galilee, Jesus passed through Samaria. Weary from the trip, the Lord sat down beside a well. When a Samaritan woman came to draw water, Jesus asked her for a drink. Surprised by his request, she inquired as to why he would ask her for a drink.

This was a very reasonable question, as there was a great deal of animosity between the Jews and the Samaritans. In fact, Jews considered Samaritans to be unclean. The fact that Jesus would visit Samaria is unusual in itself, but his request to share a drink with a Samaritan woman is even more radical. The Lord's actions serve as a reminder of just how far he will go to reach out to us. Nobody is beyond his merciful love.

From the ensuing conversation, we learn that the woman was living in a state of sin. She had five previous husbands, and Jesus bluntly informed her that "he whom you now have is not your husband" (John 4:18). Obviously, the woman was greatly in need of some intervention from Christ, and he was more than willing to get involved.

The encounter between Jesus and the Samaritan woman is fascinating reading. They start out discussing earthly water and end up talking about the "living water" known as sancti-fying grace. Essentially, it is a story of conversion; we can see the woman growing closer to the Lord. Initially, she refers to Jesus respectfully as "Sir" (John 4:15). As the conversation progresses, she recognizes him as a "prophet" (John 4:19), then as the "Christ" (John 4:29). Finally, by John 4:42, it's clear that she and the crowd questioning her acknowledge Jesus as the "Savior of the world"!

Another striking thing about this story is the fact that the woman didn't keep her newly found relationship with Christ all to herself. Her personal relationship with the Lord manifested itself in a desire to share him with others. She became an evan-gelist! Just like the apostles, who left their nets when called by Jesus, the Samaritan woman left her water jar (see John 4:28) in order to spread the Good News to others. That's what an encounter with Jesus can do!

### ZACCHAEUS (LUKE 19:1–10)

Zacchaeus was a wealthy tax collector who lived in Jericho. In the Lord's day, tax collectors were not held in high regard; in fact, they had a dishonest reputation. Most people wanted nothing to do with them. As we have seen many times, however, Jesus didn't behave the way "most people" did.

As Jesus passed through Jericho one day, Zacchaeus was interested in seeing him but ran into some difficulties. The great crowds and his lack of height made it hard for the tax collector to get a glimpse of the Lord. Did he stop there? No way! Zacchaeus climbed a sycamore tree to get a better view. And his desire to see Jesus was rewarded in a big way.

As Jesus passed the sycamore tree where the curious tax collector was perched, he cried out: "Zacchaeus, make haste and come down; for I must stay at your house today" (Luke 19:5).

Can you imagine what went through the mind of Zacchaeus? All he wanted to do was get a better look at Jesus, and now he was going to receive a private audience with him. But this is how the Lord works. If we give him a chance, he is more than willing to do whatever is necessary to help us know him better.

Wisely, Zacchaeus came down from the tree and "received him joyfully" (Luke 19:6), much to the chagrin of the crowd, who didn't approve of Jesus's associating with sinners. It's a good thing for us that the Lord doesn't feel that way. He is always willing to enter into a close relationship with sinners like us, as long as we're willing.

Zacchaeus was willing. In fact, he was more than willing. He was open to all that an encounter with Jesus offers, and his words show us that he was indeed changed on that day in Jericho: "Behold, Lord, the half of my goods I give to the poor; and if I have defrauded any one of anything, I restore it four-fold" (Luke 19:8).

There you have it: another life changed profoundly due to a "chance" encounter with Jesus.

## THE WOMAN WITH A HEMORRHAGE (MARK 5:25–34)

Are you frustrated with some of the problems in your life? Does it seem as if things will never get better? Before you give up, you need to take a look at the story of a woman who hung in there. As you'll see, her persistence truly paid off!

Can you imagine suffering from an ailment for twelve years, spending all of your money on physicians, and not getting better but getting worse? That's exactly what happened to this woman who was suffering from a persistent hemorrhage. As bad as this plight sounds, her situation was worse. The fact that she was suffering from chronic blood flow meant that she was legally unclean. As a result, she was isolated from the rest of society.

This situation could have caused the woman to lose hope, but she chose another route. Hearing the reports about Jesus, she determined that she could be healed if she could just touch his garment. And she got her chance. When she simply touched the hem of Jesus's clothing, the hemorrhage stopped, and she was healed. Just like that.

It's interesting to note how the woman approached Jesus. She didn't demand a healing; she didn't complain; she didn't even tell Jesus that she had no money. Rather, she approached him from behind and simply touched his garment (see Mark 5:27). She wasn't looking to make a scene but was turning to the Lord humbly and anonymously.

Just as Zacchaeus learned, this woman found out that there's no such thing as anonymity when it comes to Jesus. He wants more than that. He wants us to know him personally and will bend over backward to reach out to us, especially when we take the first step. Ignoring the vast crowd, Jesus turned around and asked who had touched him.

Falling down before him "in fear and trembling" (Mark 5:33), the woman confessed that she had touched him. Jesus's words must have been music to her ears: "Daughter, your faith has made you well; go in peace, and be healed of your disease" (Mark 5:34).

Sometimes we think that Jesus doesn't care about our "little" problems. Sometimes we think that our feeble prayers aren't good enough for him. Sometimes we feel as if he doesn't even notice us. This story of the woman with the hemorrhage proves that he does care, and even the briefest encounter with him can be life changing.

## THE PARALYTIC (LUKE 5:17–26)

As powerful as a relationship with Jesus can be, not everyone knows how to make the initial encounter with the Lord happen. Sometimes people need help. We'll never know what the story was for a paralytic brought to Jesus by his friends one day, but we do know the end result. Not only was the man healed, but his healing brought many people closer to the Lord.

The story begins with Jesus teaching, surrounded by Pharisees, teachers of the Law, and a great crowd of people. Suddenly, several men approached the crowd, carrying a bed containing a paralytic. A couple of things stand out. First of all, the men carrying the bed had to believe in the healing power of Jesus. Second, they had to be good friends of the paralytic in order to put forth this much effort for him.

Because of the many people surrounding the Lord, the friends had to get creative in order to facilitate the encounter between Jesus and the paralytic. They climbed up on the roof and lowered the bed before the Lord (see Luke 5:19). We know nothing about the faith of the paralytic, but we do know about the faith of his friends, who were determined to bring their friend in contact with Jesus. "And when he saw their faith he said, 'Man, your sins are forgiven you'" (Luke 5:20).

Not surprisingly, the scribes and Pharisees took issue with this, questioning Jesus's authority to forgive sins. Addressing their skepticism, the Lord explained that spiritual healings are more important than physical healings. And in an attempt to wake them up, he went ahead and healed the man's paralysis as well. He instructed the man to rise, take up his bed, and go home. "And immediately he rose before them, and took up that on which he lay, and went home, glorifying God" (Luke 5:25).

What kind of impact did this encounter with Jesus have on the crowd? "Amazement seized them all, and they glorified God and were filled with awe, saying, 'We have seen strange things today'" (Luke 5:26).

Sounds as if this encounter had an impact, don't you think?

### Bartimaeus (Mark 10:46–52)

As the saying goes, "Some things never change." There never seems to be a shortage of people who think you are crazy to trust in God. Even "believers" have their limits. While they will accept the fact that the Lord can change hearts or bring good out of a bad situation, many individuals remain skeptical about God's ability to heal or do the impossible.

Bartimaeus was a blind beggar who lived in Jericho. One day, while sitting at the side of the road, he heard that Jesus was passing by. He immediately cried out: "Jesus, Son of David, have mercy on me!" (Mark 10:47).

The people told him to be silent, but the hopeful beggar refused and repeated his cry for help. Hearing the blind man's plea, Jesus stopped and asked the crowd to "call him." In an amazing act of fickleness, the crowd urged Bartimaeus to rise and go to Jesus. Wasting no time, the blind beggar threw off his coat, sprang up, and approached the Lord. When asked what he would like Jesus to do for him, Bartimaeus replied, "Master, let me receive my sight" (Mark 10:51).

The Lord granted the request. He informed the beggar that "his faith" made him well. Immediately Bartimaeus received his sight and followed Jesus.

Take another look at the words spoken by Bartimaeus. Even if we take into account the fact that the beggar repeated himself, the number of words he spoke is less than thirty. Once again, the encounter with Jesus is more important than the quantity of words spoken.

Despite the fact that the crowd told Bartimaeus to be quiet, the blind man persisted, because he knew the power of Christ. Can you imagine the blessings that await us if we learn to ignore the cynics and become beggars before the Lord?

## THE GOOD THIEF (LUKE 23:39–43)

Did you ever get the feeling that you missed your chance in life? Maybe you feel that you're too old to love and serve the Lord. After all, everyone knows that you can't teach an old dog new tricks. While that may be a popular saying, it's absolutely not true when it comes to a relationship with Jesus. As long as you're alive, it's never too late to grow closer to Jesus!

As Jesus was being crucified, two criminals hung on crosses next to him (see Luke 23:33). One of the men lashed out at Jesus, saying, "Are you not the Christ? Save yourself and us!" (Luke 23:39). Hardly a humble prayer, right? It sounds more like a demand than a plea for help.

On the other hand, the man often referred to as "the good thief" rebuked his cohort and reminded him that there was a reason that they were being crucified. He accepted responsibility for his actions. Then, turning toward Jesus, he uttered the humble prayer familiar to many of us: "Jesus, remember me when you come in your kingly power" (Luke 23:42).

We all know what happened next. Jesus assured the repentant thief that he would indeed be with him in paradise. If there was ever an example of the fact that it's never too late to approach Jesus and ask to be his friend, this is it.

We see two men here who had an equal chance to be saved. One of them wasted the opportunity. The other ran into the arms of the Lord. How will you respond?

We could discuss many more biblical examples of people who encountered Jesus, but I think you get the idea. Meeting Jesus personally can be a life-changing experience. You and I are no different from any of the individuals examined in this chapter. We have the same opportunity to meet Jesus that each of them did. All that's required of us is to have an open mind and to approach him with humility and sincerity.

In the next chapter, we'll learn how to get started. And rest assured, the steps we need to take will be amazingly easy!

Don't Forget...

1. Even the briefest encounter with Jesus can be life changing.
2. In order for us to benefit from our meeting with the Lord, we must approach him with openness and humility.
3. Jesus knows each of us intimately and always hears us when we speak to him.
4. Don't be surprised or intimidated when people are cynical about the power of Christ and the possibility of becoming close friends with him.
5. It's never too late to accept Jesus's offer of friendship.

Jesus Says...

"Come to me, all who labor and are heavy laden, and I will give you rest." (Matthew 11:28)

## chapter five

## Ten Steps That Will Change Your Life

* * *

*Jesus Christ is the same yesterday and today and forever.*
—Hebrews 13:8

Now that we've examined some *whys* about having a relationship with Jesus, it's time to look at the *hows*. In this chapter, we'll preview the ten amazingly easy steps that will bring you and Jesus closer together—and change your life. Note that I stated that these steps are amazingly easy and will change your life. I specifically chose to use these words because they are 100 percent true.

First, every one of these steps is easy to implement. I'm not going to force you to become a Scripture scholar, attend a thirty-day retreat, or preach on a street corner. Instead, I will ask you to do things that you can begin today, in your own home, with readily available aids.

Which brings me to the second point: Don't let the simplicity of the steps fool you into doubting their effectiveness. How can I be so sure that following these steps will change your life? I have seen them work in my life and the lives of others, so it's safe to say that they will work in yours as well.

While I may not know you personally, I do know Jesus, and I know how he can transform lives. In the last chapter, we looked at several individuals who had encounters with Jesus, all of them life changing. If you practice these steps and remain open to the movement of the Holy Spirit, you will not only become closer friends with Jesus, but your life will be transformed. He really is that powerful.

We will devote a section to each of the ten amazingly easy steps to a closer friendship with Jesus, but first let's have a brief overview.

### Step One: Break Down the Walls

Why is it that so many individuals (even those who regularly attend Mass) don't have a close, personal relationship with Jesus? For one thing, it sounds like a Protestant idea, so many Catholics aren't comfortable with the concept. Another obstacle is that it's difficult to be friends with someone whom we can't see or hear in a traditional way. Many of us also struggle with the idea of making time for Jesus. This is particularly true for those of us who are very busy or who dislike sitting for any length of time. When you throw selfishness and fear of suffering into the mix, there are many barriers that hold us back from a deeper relationship with the Lord. In the next section, we will discuss various walls that prevent us from growing closer to Jesus and offer suggestions for breaking them down.

### Step Two: Let the Church Guide You

Sometimes Christians put so much emphasis on having a personal relationship with Jesus that they ignore the Church that he gave us in order to nourish that relationship. The "me and Jesus" mentality just isn't sound. Jesus founded a Church, and our personal relationship with him must exist as part of his Church.

Although many Catholics experience the opposite problem (more focus on going to church than on establishing a personal relationship with Christ), I have to address this topic so that the pursuit of a deeper relationship with Jesus doesn't drive anyone away from the Church. In fact, a healthy relationship with Jesus should draw us closer to his Church. St. Paul teaches that the Church is the body of Christ. "For by one Spirit we were all baptized into one body—Jews or Greeks, slaves or free—and all were made to drink of one Spirit" (1 Corinthians 12:13). "Now you are the body of Christ and individually members of it" (1 Corinthians 12:27).

STEP THREE: TALK TO JESUS

What is prayer? Many individuals think of it as asking God for what they need. While that is certainly a valid form of prayer, it is incomplete. Prayer is essentially a conversation with the Lord.

In any relationship, communication is essential. If we want to have a close, personal relationship with Jesus, we must pray every day.

Furthermore, prayer is always effective. Every time we pray, something happens. While it may not always be what we want, there is always some fruit that comes from our prayers.

In step 3, we will discuss the importance of conversing with the Lord on a daily basis (even when we don't feel like it), explore different methods of prayer (some of which are so simple that we may not feel as if we're praying), and offer easy-to-follow suggestions for fitting prayer into our busy lives.

STEP FOUR: LISTEN!

The Church clearly states that it is possible to hear the Lord speak. In the Vatican II document *Dei Verbum,* we read that "we speak to Him when we pray; we hear Him when we read the divine saying."[4] Make no mistake about it: Every time we open the Bible, the Lord speaks to us! While it's not the only way that he speaks, it's definitely the most reliable way. We may doubt if the thought or feeling that we're receiving in prayer is actually coming from the Lord, but there is no doubt that he inspired every word contained in the Bible.

Sacred Scripture can sometimes be confusing and intimidating. Even though the Lord may be speaking, we may not know how to listen. In step 4, we'll look at some techniques that will help us to hear the voice of Jesus though the pages of the Bible. After exploring this topic, it will be very difficult for you to say, "God doesn't speak to me"!

## STEP FIVE: GO FOR THE GRACE

The *Catechism of the Catholic Church* states that Christ "is present in the sacraments" and that "when anybody baptizes, it is really Christ himself who baptizes" (*CCC* 1088). Therefore, if we want to encounter Jesus, it only makes sense that we use the sacraments.

Although we'll give special attention in step 5 to the Eucharist (in which Christ is present in the fullest way possible), each of the sacraments allows us to have an encounter with the Lord. These encounters (and the grace that flows from them) help us to grow closer to Jesus and know him more intimately.

## STEP SIX: ENJOY HIS REAL PRESENCE

Jesus Christ is the best friend that you and I could ever have, and he waits for us in churches and chapels around the world. Eucharistic Adoration is a wonderful opportunity to spend quality time with the Lord. In this case, absence doesn't make the heart grow fonder. If we want to grow closer to Jesus, spending time with him is essential.

Let's face it: We all have bad days from time to time. When we're feeling down, nothing can lift our spirits like an unexpected call from a close friend. As uplifting as this experience can be, however, there is something even better—a personal visit! In the company of a close friend, our worries and cares seem to drift away. Even if the friend is unable to help us with our problems, his or her companionship is a great gift.

The thought of spending time in the presence of Jesus can be intimidating. We are often confused about what to say or do. In step 6, we'll discuss how to make it easier, but here's something we should always remember: While we sit with Jesus, he is also reaching out to us, even if we don't hear or feel him. In other words, we're not doing all the work! Time spent in the presence of Christ is never wasted. It will always help us grow closer to him.

STEP SEVEN: LET MOM HELP!

While Jesus was dying on the cross, he presented us with a great gift. Unlike the gifts we typically receive, this gift is not an object; it is a person! Looking at his mother and the "disciple whom he loved" (generally accepted as John), Jesus uttered the famous words, "Woman, behold your son!" Then turning to the disciple, Jesus said, "Behold, your mother!" (John 19:26, 27). At that moment, you and I received a spiritual mother— Mary. Her job is to help us grow closer to her Son.

In step 7, we'll look at some of the events in Mary's life, including her role at the wedding at Cana and her presence at the foot of the cross. Additionally, we'll tackle the common fear that Marian devotion will take us away from Jesus. In reality, this is not true at all. Mary's role is to lead us to Jesus, not away from him! As our spiritual mother, that is exactly what she will do—if we give her permission.

### STEP EIGHT: LOVE YOUR NEIGHBOR

Jesus was extremely clear when he said, "Truly, I say to you, as you did it to one of the least of these my brethren, you did it to me" (Matthew 25:40). Simply put, the way we treat our neighbor is the way we treat Jesus. If we're kind to everyone we meet, we are being kind to the Lord. If we're mean or uncaring, then we're being mean or uncaring to Jesus. Taking a broader look at this concept, we encounter Jesus in everyone we meet!

We often forget about the Lord's powerful words regarding love of neighbor. This is especially true when it comes to individuals whom we label as "difficult" or "undesirable." Yet, if we are to have a close personal relationship with Jesus Christ, we'll need to see him in everyone—including our enemies. Even though it can be challenging, accepting and acting upon this fact is necessary for growing close to him. We'll talk more about this in step 8.

### STEP NINE: SEEK AND FIND

As we go through the day dealing with problems and responsibilities, it's very easy to forget about the Lord. The fact that we can't see him with our eyes and hear him with our ears makes us lose sight of the fact that he is always with us. From an early age, we have been trained to rely on our senses to process the world around us. The inability to use them to perceive the Lord can be challenging, but it can be overcome.

What happens when we can't see something (like air) or someone (like Jesus)? Instead of simply forgetting about him, we can learn to find him in everything we do. Although this requires some training and involves looking at things in a different way, it is totally achievable. In step 9, we'll discuss some practical and easy ways to find Jesus in the midst of our daily activities.

## STEP TEN: DON'T WASTE YOUR SUFFERING

No matter how we may try to escape it, suffering is (and always will be) a part of our lives. But don't let that bring you down. Consider this: Suffering can bring you closer to Christ. Furthermore, when you unite your suffering to the suffering of Jesus, it is possible to experience great peace in the midst of it.

In addition to the fact that we have a tendency to run from suffering, we sometimes have trouble recognizing it. Suffering doesn't always come in big packages. Even our minor crosses (such as tiredness and traffic jams) can unite us more closely with the Lord. These too we can offer up for God's purposes. In step 10, we'll look at suffering and its redemptive value.

As we prepare to dig into the ten amazingly easy steps to a closer friendship with the Lord, I'd like to share some words of Pope Francis:

> I invite all Christians, everywhere, at this very moment, to
> a renewed personal encounter with Jesus Christ, or at least
> an openness to letting him encounter them; I ask all of you
> to do this unfailingly each day. No one should think that
> this invitation is not meant for him or her, since "no one
> is excluded from the joy brought by the Lord." The Lord

does not disappoint those who take this risk; whenever we take a step towards Jesus, we come to realize that he is already there, waiting for us with open arms.[5]

Will you accept the Holy Father's invitation? I hope so, because Jesus is waiting. It is possible to have a personal relationship with Jesus and to do so now!

DON'T FORGET...

1. There are steps you can begin today that will help you grow closer to Jesus.
2. These steps are amazingly easy.
3. It is entirely possible to encounter Jesus in all of our daily activities.
4. Remaining close to Christ always results in increased peace.
5. All Christians are invited to have a personal encounter with Jesus Christ.

JESUS SAYS...

"Follow me." (Mark 2:14)

## step one Break Down the Walls

* » ⚬

Indeed I count everything as loss because of the surpassing
worth of knowing Christ Jesus my Lord.
—Philippians 3:8

If friendship with Jesus has so many benefits, why is it
that so many of us resist or struggle with establishing that
relationship?

In all honesty, there are many obstacles that can prevent us
from having a close personal friendship with the Lord. If not
addressed, these issues can make a relationship with Jesus seem
impossible. We can end up surrounded by walls that keep us
away from the Lord.

The good news is that you can deal with the walls in your
life and draw closer to Christ. Some walls will crumble easily;
others might require more work. In some cases, the walls are so
firm that it might be easier just to leave them in place and climb
over them. But none of these walls need to keep you away from
a close relationship with Jesus.

What matters is that we learn to address the obstacles that are
keeping us from growing closer to the Lord. Let's look at some
of the big ones and explore practical ways to overcome them.

## SEEING IS BELIEVING

From an early age, we are trained to believe what we see. Generally speaking, if we can see something with our eyes, we tend to believe that it exists. Since Jesus cannot be seen with our eyes (at least in the typical way), we often struggle to believe that he is real and that it's possible to have a relationship with him.

*Solution:* We are surrounded by many things that definitely exist but are invisible. Air, atoms, natural gas, and electricity can't be seen with our eyes, yet we accept the fact that they are real. There are no photographs of George Washington, but I've yet to meet a person who doesn't believe he existed. Why is it that we believe in some things that we can't see but not others?

Much of it has to do with the way we think. We tend to more readily believe scientific or historical facts than supernatural concepts. Most people have no problem believing that Christ was born two thousand years ago, but the idea that he is just as alive today as he was then is a difficult one to accept.

The easiest way to eliminate this obstacle is to talk to Jesus and ask for help. Since Jesus *is* real, he will respond to your request, and your faith will grow. It might take some getting used to, but you'll start to feel his presence. That's because of the fact that he'll be working too. Once you give him the permission to enter more deeply into your life, he will do just that. Even though he will remain invisible, you'll know that he exists. That's what the amazing power of faith can do!

## THE WEIRDNESS FACTOR

For most people, it just feels strange talking to someone who can't be seen and heard. Jesus can seem like an imaginary friend. And we all know that supposedly normal people don't have relationships with imaginary friends. Furthermore, many Catholics are uncomfortable with the whole concept of having a personal relationship with Jesus. It sounds way too Protestant. We just don't do that.

*Solution:* Although this obstacle manifests itself differently than does the first one, the solution is the same. The best way to conquer the weirdness factor is to start speaking to Jesus and see what happens. Since he is real (even though our senses may tell us otherwise), we will be in the position of the people we studied in chapter 4—Zacchaeus, the woman at the well, the apostles, and so on.

Even though it might feel strange at first, as time progresses, you'll care less about any feelings of strangeness and more about the benefits. You will even reach a point where you want to tell others about your friend Jesus. The fact that they don't care or that they think that you're weird will probably not even cross your mind!

### Silence Isn't Always Golden

How in the world can we have a conversation, let alone a friendship, with a person who never speaks? This is a very real problem. Barring any miraculous exceptions, we are never going to hear Jesus speak in an audible way, and that can be a deal breaker for a potential friendship.

*Solution:* It may be a tired cliché, but we need to think outside of the box. Jesus speaks frequently, but not in the traditional way. In order to hear his voice, we need to learn to listen.

One of the most reliable ways to hear the Lord speak is by reading the Bible. Since the Church teaches that the Bible was written under the inspiration of the Holy Spirit, we can be assured that the Lord speaks to us through Sacred Scripture. Does this take some getting used to? Absolutely! We'll discuss how the Lord speaks to us through the Bible in step 4. For now, just know that he does.

Jesus also speaks to us through the teachings of the Church, through other people, through circumstances, through nature, through our thoughts, and through our feelings. Believe me, if we learn to listen in these ways, we will hear his voice—loud and clear.

NOT ENOUGH TIME

In today's world, people are busy—very busy! It often feels as if there aren't enough hours in the day to get everything done. As we run around, balancing family and work obligations, quiet time with Jesus can seem impossible. Maybe we could work on it if we had more time. But for now, considering all the things that absolutely have to get done, it's just not realistic.

*Solution:* There is an amazingly easy fix to this problem. We need to carve out some time for Jesus in our daily lives. This might be a little painful to accept, but we always make time for things that are important to us. If we don't have time to spend with the Lord, then it's obviously not that important to us.

Those of us who are parents know what it's like to leave work for a few hours to attend a school event or to buy supplies for a birthday party. We do these things not necessarily because we feel like it but out of love. If we love our spouse, we always seem to find the time to drop what we're doing and spend some time together.

Our relationship with Jesus works the same way. If we are too busy for him, we will never get to know him personally. Don't know how to start? Ten minutes as soon as you wake up and ten minutes just before going to bed would be a great beginning! I have plenty more about prayer in step 3.

## IT'S NOT POSSIBLE

Even though we hear the phrase "personal relationship with Jesus" all the time, many people feel it's not possible to know him personally. Are you one of those?

*Solution:* This is a tricky one. If I countered the argument by assuring you that it is possible to become close friends with the Lord, you might not believe me. But I'm going to say it anyway! Let me assure you that it is indeed possible to have a personal relationship with Jesus. Furthermore, it is possible for *you* to have that relationship.

If you're skeptical (and you may very well be), my reassurance probably won't be enough to change your mind. Therefore, I'm asking you to give it a try and see what happens. Obviously, you're interested in getting to know Jesus, or you wouldn't be reading this book. You're off to a great start!

I guarantee that if you practice the steps in this book, you'll discover for yourself that it is entirely possible to have a personal relationship with Jesus. I will also guarantee that once you get to know him closely, you'll never want to go back to the way things used to be.

## A THING OF THE PAST

Since Jesus Christ is a historical figure who lived two thousand years ago, we sometimes treat him the way we treat other deceased individuals. For many people, the thought of having a conversation with Christ is about as realistic as having a conversation with Abraham Lincoln or Martin Luther King, Jr.

We may have read about their lives, but knowing them is not regarded as feasible.

*Solution:* Fortunately for us, Jesus Christ is very much alive and wants to converse with us frequently. We do have to be careful, however, that we don't fall into a common trap. When we read about Jesus in the Gospels, we shouldn't treat what we read like a history lesson. Even though we are learning about events and hearing quotes that took place two thousand years ago, the Bible is not an ordinary book.

Reading the autobiography of Mark Twain will allow me to read his words and learn about his life, but it doesn't give me the chance to ask him questions. If he wrote something I didn't understand, I can spend time contemplating it, but I can't ask him to elaborate. On the other hand, when I open my Bible and read about Jesus, I can have a conversation with him. I can ask questions about suffering and how it applies to my life. I can ask Jesus what it felt like to agonize in the garden on the night before he died. I can tell him that I'm struggling to appreciate heaven and ask him to help me.

Although I might have to practice listening and learn to be patient, Jesus will respond to my queries. The Jesus who lived two thousand years ago and now resides in heaven is still very much with us—he just looks a little different!

## Too Much Competition

Did you ever try to read a book while watching TV or listening to music? It may be possible to do some light reading under these conditions, but it generally doesn't work well for academic study. Noise makes it difficult to concentrate.

We live in a very noisy world and are constantly bombarded with distractions. How is it possible to hear Jesus speak when we can barely hear ourselves think?

*Solution:* For the most part, Jesus speaks in silence or in ways that require concentration. As a result, this obstacle can be very challenging. As with so many of these solutions, we definitely need to do some work. And although the answer is simple, it can be difficult to put into practice.

There is no getting around the fact that we will never get to know Jesus if we don't spend some quiet time with him. If we're really serious about entering into a relationship with him, we need to turn off the TV, radio, or iPod and let him speak to us. Even though it may seem painful at first, the end result will be well worth the effort.

### ME, ME, ME

As a general rule, most individuals are primarily concerned with their own wants, needs, and problems. While this is not always a bad thing (we should be aware of our needs and problems), it can get in the way of a close personal relationship with Jesus. If we spend too much time thinking about what we need, we're not going to care about what he needs.

All too often, we view the Lord as a vending machine. We approach him when we're in need, drop a few coins (prayers) in the slot, and expect to instantly receive our answer. True friendship means putting your friend's needs before your own. Unless we discover a way to counter the "me, me, me" mentality, we will not have a meaningful relationship with the Lord.

*Solution:* The first step to overcoming this obstacle is to recognize that it is a problem. Many times we don't even realize that we're overly concerned about our own needs. Even if you pray every day, you might still be affected by this mentality. How can you tell?

Take a look at your prayers, particularly the order of your requests. Do you pray for yourself before you pray for others? Do you ever ask the Lord what you can do for him, or do you spend most of your prayer time telling him what you need?

If you see a problem here, it's one that's very easy to fix. By changing the order of your petitions and telling the Lord you're at his service, you will put the needs of others before your own.

Also, try meditating on the Lord's passion. It is a very effective way to overcome this obstacle. Before long, you'll find yourself thinking less about your needs and more about how much Jesus loves you.

### "I Can't Let Go"

Many people find it difficult to give up control of their lives, even to the Lord. This can be a problem, especially if we try to control the uncontrollable. In fact, the desire for control is one of the greatest sources of anxiety in the world today. When we refuse to accept the fact that some things are beyond our control, it can cause us constant worry.

This has always been a struggle for me. Yet I have come to realize that my friendship with Jesus will be impeded by any failure to turn my life over to him. I want to be friends with the Lord, so I need to find ways to trust him—even when things don't go my way.

*Solution:* Although this is one of those walls that you may not be able to completely demolish, it's one that you can learn to scale on a regular basis. Jesus wants us to trust him with our lives. He expects us to do what we can to fix the problems that we encounter, but he also wants us to yield control to him once we've done all we can.

How can we overcome this desire to remain in control? The first and easiest step is to ask the Lord to help us trust him. This one is so basic that it is often overlooked.

The next thing is to trust him with the things you can't change. If something unpleasant happens (a flat tire, a traffic jam, an upset stomach, an exchange with a difficult coworker, or even a major catastrophe), try thanking Jesus for allowing it. Since these events are going to happen anyway, you may as well learn to accept them. Doing so will bring you great peace.

Eventually, with the Lord's help, you will find yourself being more open to his will in your life. And that will help your relationship with him to flourish.

Although there could be additional barriers that stand between you and Jesus, eliminating the ones covered in this section will greatly improve your ability to have a close, personal relationship with him.

But before you get swept up with the thought that Jesus is all you need, we're going to shift gears and look at the dangers of having a "just me and Jesus" mentality. While it's absolutely true that Jesus wants to be our best friend, we need to recognize the importance of the Church in that relationship. We'll discuss that in the next section.

Don't Forget...

1. There are many walls that can block us from moving closer to Jesus, but all of them can be knocked down or climbed over.

2. One major obstacle is the fact that we can't see or hear Jesus in the traditional way.

3. It is definitely possible to hear the Lord speak, but it requires some work on our part.

4. Once we ask Jesus for help, many of these walls come tumbling down more easily than we expect. That's because he's doing much of the work!

5. Yielding control of our lives to the Lord is often one of the walls that can't be completely destroyed, but it can be scaled.

Jesus Says...

"Blessed are those who have not seen and yet believe." (John 20:29)

## step two  Let the Church Guide You

I hope to come to you soon, but I am writing these instructions so that, if I am delayed, you may know how one ought to behave in the household of God, which is the Church of the living God, the pillar and bulwark of the truth.

— 1 TIMOTHY 3:14–15

Having a personal relationship with Jesus is a very good thing—so good, in fact, that some want to run away with him to a deserted island. But this "just me and Jesus" way of thinking can lead us away from the Lord if we're not careful. A close, personal relationship with Jesus can only be fully experienced through the Church.

How can we avoid this potential booby trap? The answer is actually quite simple. Don't forget the Church!

I DID IT MY WAY

For most of my professional life, I was employed as a computer programmer. I started out working for a software company designing products for business use and eventually moved to a firm that developed software for naval weapons systems. As you can probably imagine, programming computers for use on ships engaged in combat was a complex process. In order to ensure that the systems worked properly, an elaborate test environment was set up. A land-based test ship was built and fitted with equipment designed to simulate the conditions at sea. There, we were able to test our programs in order to identify potential problems.

In addition to the special test facility, we were also able to test the software at our desks. While not as elaborate as the test site, the simulators my company designed for our desktop computers were a blessing. I preferred working in my comfortable office instead of a dark, cold, highly secured building, which really did look like a ship. Unfortunately, this desire for comfort led to a painful experience—one that I never saw coming.

I was working on some complicated computer software that would display various system statuses on large screens located throughout the ship. After receiving my assignment, I felt that I knew how to proceed. Fortunately for me, my work could be tested right in my office. Even though it was recommended that we periodically verify our results at the test site, I opted for the convenience of my office.

As the weeks passed, I was feeling very good about the progress I was making. All of the pieces seemed to be coming together, and my deadline was still a few weeks away. As I entered the final week before my project was due, I determined that it was time to pay a visit to the test site. Once my work was officially tested, I could lean back and relax a bit.

Upon arriving at the test facility and loading my software, I was stunned with what I saw. Nothing worked. And when I say nothing, I mean nothing! All of the status displays were completely blank.

My initial reaction was that this must be a hardware problem, but a brief discussion with a fellow developer showed that the problem was my fault. All of my work had been based on a faulty assumption. If I had visited the test site earlier, I would have uncovered this problem. Now I had to give my boss the bad news that I would not be able to complete the project on time. As a result, my company would not be able to deliver the software to the government by the date specified in the contract.

This was a very bad thing. I didn't lose my job, but my reputation within the company was damaged. I learned that operating in a vacuum can lead to many problems. Not only does this concept apply to our professional or personal life but to our spiritual life as well.

## Jesus's Instrument

Fortunately for us, Jesus understands human nature very well. He knows that we have a tendency to become overly comfortable. He also recognizes that we tend to overlook our imperfections and sinfulness. In order to protect us from ourselves, Christ founded the Catholic Church. And through his Church, we can not only meet him personally but make it to heaven. The Church serves to connect all of mankind with God and with one another.

> The Church's first purpose is to be the sacrament of the *inner union of men with God*. Because men's communion with one another is rooted in that union with God, the Church is also the sacrament of the *unity of the human race*. In her, this unity is already begun, since she gathers men "from every nation, from all tribes and peoples and

tongues"; at the same time, the Church is the "sign and instrument" of the full realization of the unity yet to come. (CCC 775, quoting Revelation 7:9)

When we enter the Church (through faith and baptism; see CCC 1267), we actually enter into intimate communion with Christ.

> From the beginning, Jesus associated his disciples with his own life, revealed the mystery of the Kingdom to them, and gave them a share in his mission, joy, and sufferings. Jesus spoke of a still more intimate communion between him and those who would follow him: "Abide in me, and I in you.... I am the vine, you are the branches" [John 16:4–5]. And he proclaimed a mysterious and real communion between his own body and ours: "He who eats my flesh and drinks my blood abides in me, and I in him" [John 6:56].
>
> When his visible presence was taken from them, Jesus did not leave his disciples orphans. He promised to remain with them until the end of time; he sent them his Spirit [see John 14:18; 20:22; Matthew 28:20; Acts 2:33]. As a result communion with Jesus has become, in a way, more intense: "By communicating his Spirit, Christ mystically constitutes as his body those brothers of his who are called together from every nation" [*Lumen Gentium* 7].
>
> The comparison of the Church with the body casts light on the intimate bond between Christ and his Church. Not only is she gathered *around him*; she is united *in him*, in his body. Three aspects of the Church as the Body of Christ are to be more specifically noted: the unity of all

her members with each other as a result of their union with Christ; Christ as head of the Body; and the Church as bride of Christ. (*CCC* 787–789)

While reading the Bible and speaking to the Lord in prayer will certainly bring us closer to him, we can't ignore the importance of his Church and her teachings. When we approach Christ solely on our own, we make the same mistake I did while working on that ill-fated computer system. We become branches that try to grow apart from the vine. Jesus reminds us what happens when we choose that approach:

> As the branch cannot bear fruit by itself, unless it abides in the vine, neither can you, unless you abide in me. I am the vine, you are the branches. He who abides in me, and I in him, he it is that bears much fruit, for apart from me you can do nothing. (John 15:4–5)

You may wonder how you can recognize that you're headed down the wrong path. Is it possible to be unintentionally moving away from Christ without realizing it?

Let's look at a few general rules of thumb: If your interpretation of Scripture conflicts with Catholic teaching, you are headed in the wrong direction. If you feel that the Lord is telling you through prayer that it's acceptable to disobey a teaching of the Church, you are wrong. Period! It really is that simple. According to the Code of Canon Law:

> To the Church belongs the right always and everywhere to announce moral principles, including those pertaining to the social order, and to make judgments on any human

affairs to the extent that they are required by the fundamental rights of the human person or the salvation of souls. (CCC 2032, quoting *Codex Iuris Canonici*, canon 747:2)

Christ founded a Church so that we wouldn't have to struggle to make it to heaven on our own. Instead of looking at Church teaching as restrictive, we should view it as a gift. Through the teaching authority of the Church, the Lord tells us what we need to do (or avoid) to become holy and get to heaven.

## Teach Me, O Lord

We live in a world where the word *law* has negative connotations. In general, people don't like to be told what to do. If we go back in time, we can see that the Israelites viewed the law much differently. Rather than looking at God's law as restrictive, they viewed it as an expression of his love. By giving us commands and guidelines to follow, the Lord actually helps us remain close to him.

This sentiment is expressed beautifully in Psalm 119. It's the longest of the psalms, and it contains a great expression of love for God's law. I strongly recommend that you read through it, but here is a brief excerpt:

> Teach me, O Lord, the way of your statutes;
> and I will keep it to the end.
> Give me understanding, that I may keep your law
> and observe it with my whole heart.
> Lead me in the paths of your commandments,
> for I delight in it. (Psalm 119:33–35)

Many Catholics fall into the trap of doing things or supporting causes that are in violation of Church teaching. This typically happens when Catholics don't know what the Church teaches. Fortunately, this problem is correctable. Catholics need only get familiar with the teachings of the Church.

One of the best resources for assistance in this is the *Catechism of the Catholic Church*. In this tremendous book, we can find a summary of two thousand years of Church teaching. Reading the *Catechism* (and using it for reference) has changed my life and drawn me closer to Jesus than ever before. We are truly blessed to have such a great summary of our Catholic faith at our fingertips.[6]

How about those individuals who claim to love Jesus but reject the concept of a visible and structured Church? As someone who went to Catholic school for twelve years and found religion to be "boring," I totally get what it's like to feel that the Church is irrelevant. I made the mistake of disassociating from his Church for years. I viewed Sunday Mass attendance (and all Church teaching) strictly as an obligation. I lost sight of the presence of Jesus in his Church and her teachings. So religion became a boring set of rules to me.

On the other hand, if we understand the fact that the Church is the Mystical Body of Christ (we'll explore that concept in step 10), we enjoy hearing the Lord speak through his Church. If we truly seek Jesus, we will find him in the Church.

In a reply to her judges, St. Joan of Arc left us with a powerful reminder: "About Jesus Christ and the Church, I simply know they're just one thing, and we shouldn't complicate the matter" (CCC 795, quoting Acts of the Trial of Joan of Arc).

Don't Forget...

1. Jesus founded his Church as the means for drawing believers into a close, personal relationship with him.
2. Christ will never give us permission to disobey a teaching of his Church.
3. Reading the Bible without considering Church teachings is a big mistake.
4. Jesus gave us the Catholic Church to help us get to heaven.
5. Church teachings are not designed to deprive us of pleasure but are expressions of God's love.

Jesus Says...

"And I tell you, you are Peter, and on this rock I will build my Church, and the gates of Hades shall not prevail against it." (Matthew 16:18)

. . .

Rejoice always, pray constantly, give thanks in all circumstances;
for this is the will of God in Christ Jesus for you.
— 1 Thessalonians 5:16–18

If we want to have a close, personal relationship with Jesus,
we must pray. There is no way around it. But what is prayer?

Prayer is not necessarily the easiest thing to define. Many
people would say that it is a way to ask God for things. That
answer is true but incomplete. Requesting favors from the Lord
is only one of several types of prayer.

The *Catechism of the Catholic Church* defines prayer with a
quote from St. John Damascene: "Prayer is the raising of one's
mind and heart to God or the requesting of good things from
God" (CCC 2559). The *Catechism* presents several different
ways to pray (see CCC 2626–2643), all of which involve an
encounter with the Lord. Let's take a look at each of them.

BLESSING AND ADORATION

Although it's typically not the first form of prayer that comes
to mind, blessing and adoration is a very important way of
communicating with the Lord. Everything we have is a gift from
God. Our very existence is due to his generosity. When we offer

prayers of blessing, we are responding to God's gifts. We are able to bless him for having blessed us.

St. Peter gives us a good example of this type of prayer:

> Blessed be the God and Father of our Lord Jesus Christ! By his great mercy we have been born anew to a living hope through the resurrection of Jesus Christ from the dead, and to an inheritance which is imperishable, undefiled, and unfading, kept in heaven for you, who by God's power are guarded through faith for a salvation ready to be revealed in the last time. (1 Peter 1:3–5)

What about prayer of adoration? When we pray in this manner, we recognize that we are creatures and God is our Creator. We think about his greatness and reflect on his infinite power. How often have you thought about this today?

Don't be too hard on yourself, as adoration is something that many of us overlook. We get so caught up in running around and taking care of problems that we forget about the Lord's incredible power. This is sad for a couple of reasons. First, we deprive the Lord of the adoration that is due him. Also, we deprive ourselves of the comfort that comes from knowing that he is bigger than all of our problems.

With the Lord, there is no such thing as an unfixable problem. This is something that I've learned to focus on frequently, especially when I'm facing a situation that seems hopeless. One of the best ways for your faith to grow is to meditate on the Lord's almighty power.

PRAYER OF PETITION

In this form of prayer, we recognize the fact that we are not self-sufficient. We have many needs, and any one of them can become the basis for a prayer of petition. We sometimes forget to pray for our lesser needs. We know where to find the Lord when we have a major catastrophe (cancer, job loss, financial difficulties), but we forget to ask him for the less obvious things (a parking spot, a solution to a problem at work, wisdom for financial decisions).

When I speak at parishes and conferences, I encourage my audiences to get in the habit of asking God for things—not just material things but spiritual things as well. Human nature being what it is, we tend to think that we have to fix everything ourselves. Even when we try to become holy, we often feel that it's necessary to grit our teeth and do it alone. What a mistake! Whether I'm trying to give up worrying or striving to overcome my favorite sin, God doesn't want me to do it by myself. He wants me to ask for help.

If you have trouble trusting God, ask for help. If you find it impossible to be kind to others, ask the Lord for help. If you're struggling to overcome lukewarmness, by all means, ask for help.

God will always answer your prayers. It may not be as fast as you would like or in the way that you expect, but you will receive an answer. On the other hand, if you don't ask...

St. James tells us, "You do not have, because you do not ask" (James 4:2).

PRAYER OF INTERCESSION

When we offer prayers for the needs of others, we imitate Jesus, who "always lives to make intercession" for us (Hebrews 7:25). We may not understand why this type of prayer is effective, but we know that it is. In addition to its effectiveness, praying for others is an act of charity.

We sometimes focus so much on our own problems that we forget to pray for others. As I mentioned earlier, pay attention to the order of your intentions. If you're praying for all of your needs first, you may be putting too much emphasis on yourself. This problem can be easily remedied by reversing the order of your prayers: Pray for others before praying for your own needs. Everyone is covered, and you become more charitable.

Throughout the Bible, we can find numerous examples of intercessory prayer. One of my favorites involves a battle between the Israelites and the Amalekites (see Exodus 17:8–13). As the battle raged at Rephidim, Moses stood at the top of a hill with the rod of God in his hand. When Moses held up his hand, Israel had the advantage. When he lowered his hand, however, Amalek prevailed. Eventually, the hands of Moses grew weary, so he was given a stone to sit upon, and Aaron and Hur held up his arms to keep them steady. As a result, Joshua and the Israelite army were able to defeat the Amalekites.

By himself, Moses was unable to keep his hands raised in a gesture of prayer. With the help of others, however, his prayers were answered. This is another great lesson for us. How often do we need the support of others in order to persevere in prayer?

## PRAYER OF THANKSGIVING AND PRAYER OF PRAISE

It's a common practice to thank others for their generosity. My parents drilled this idea into my head at a young age, and I'm glad that they did. When at times I would forget to express my gratitude to others, I would hear the familiar question, "What do you say?"

Sometimes we're better at thanking those we see around us than at thanking the Lord. Every day of my fifty-plus years on this earth has been a gift from God, but I shudder to think about how few times I have thanked him. My negligence has not been intentional but primarily due to a lack of awareness.

I now start my day by thanking the Lord for letting me wake up. I then try to recall the many other things that I'm grateful for and proceed to thank him for them. The list is very long—my family, my job, my home, my car, the fact that I can worship him freely, his presence in the Eucharist, the sacraments, my redemption, and so on. If I put my mind to it each day, I can think of dozens of things to be thankful for. If I don't set aside the time to think about it, however, I'll overlook most of them.

One thing that we rarely thank God for is suffering. It seems completely counterintuitive to do so. Why in the world should we be thankful for something that is so painful? It makes no sense.

In reality, however, suffering is a great gift, as it can help get us and many others to heaven. If we can learn to ignore our feelings (this can be challenging) and thank the Lord for the suffering that he allows us to experience, we can definitely grow spiritually. St. Thérèse of Lisieux revealed a profound understanding of this in her autobiography:

> And so, in spite of this trial which robs me of all sense of pleasure, I can still say: "Thou hast given me, O Lord, a delight in all Thy doings." For is there any greater joy than to suffer for love of You? The more intense and hidden the suffering is, the more pleasing it is to You. And if—which is impossible—You knew nothing of it, I should still be happy to suffer in the hope that, by my tears, I could prevent or perhaps atone for a single sin against the Faith.[7]

We'll say more about the gift of suffering in step 10.

We offer prayers of praise when we give the Lord glory simply because he is God. Unlike the previous ways of praying that we've discussed, this type of prayer is not based on any of the Lord's accomplishments or gifts to us. It simply involves acknowledging his magnificence as the Supreme Being. According to the *Catechism*, prayer of praise gives glory to God "because HE IS" (*CCC* 2649). Although it is a very basic form of prayer, it is extremely powerful and can help us keep things in perspective.

## GETTING BEYOND THE COMFORT ZONE

Now that we have discussed several different ways to pray, which one should we use? All of them! Each day we should get into the habit of adoring, blessing, thanking, and praising the Lord. In addition, we should ask for our needs and the needs of others. If we don't force ourselves (yes, force ourselves!) to use these different forms of prayer, our prayer can become very comfortable but stale. That is not a good thing. Eventually we might find ourselves merely going through the motions.

Here's an analogy that comes to mind. When I was growing up, I wanted to learn how to play the guitar. I was a big music fan, and I wanted to play just as my favorite musicians did. My parents bought me a guitar, and I started to take music lessons.

Unfortunately, I was impatient and didn't have time for all of that music theory stuff. I wanted to play songs, not waste time learning the proper way to play. As a result, I stopped working on learning how to read music and focused on what I enjoyed—playing songs by ear. And even though I did end up playing professionally when I got older, I was always weak at reading music. This weakness held me back and made learning new songs very difficult.

My tendency to get comfortable also got in the way in my twenties when I decided to start lifting weights. As do many bodybuilders, I made the mistake of concentrating on my arms and upper body and neglected working on my legs. Working the lower body was difficult and, in my opinion, wasn't worth the effort. As a result of the lack of balance in my workout, however, my body started to grow out of proportion.

When we pray, the easiest thing to say is "Gimme!" Unless we make a conscious effort to use several types of prayer, we will most likely end up doing what is easiest—asking for things. While it's fine to ask the Lord for what we need, we don't want it to be the only thing we do. Can you imagine treating your other friends in that way?

No friendship will last if we only communicate when we need something. And prayer is communication with our best friend, God. If we incorporate all of the above techniques into our prayers, that relationship with the Lord will grow by leaps and bounds. The end result will be worth the effort.

While we're on the subject of making conscious decisions on how to pray, let's address the number-one threat to our prayer life—lack of feeling. How many times have you not prayed because you didn't feel like it? If you're like most of the world, it has probably happened. We tend to pursue things that feel good and shy away from things that are painful. Approaching the spiritual life in that way can lead to mediocrity.

No matter how close you become with Jesus, there will be days when you don't feel like praying. It could be due to the fact that you're tired, not feeling well, preoccupied with problems— or any number of reasons. You can take comfort in the fact that it's perfectly normal to feel that way at times. It doesn't mean that you don't love Jesus or that you're a bad person. It simply means that you're human. Feelings are neither right nor wrong.

In fact, the Church teaches that feelings (or emotions) are morally neutral. Your actions are what matter. If you pray when you don't feel like it, you are showing the Lord just how much you love him.

My wife and I woke up many times to change diapers or comfort our children when they were infants. We didn't do it because it felt good; we did it because we loved them. If you want to have a close personal relationship with Jesus, you must pray every day—even when you don't feel like it. There are no exceptions to this rule.

EVERYDAY PRAYER

The most important thing I can tell you about prayer is to make sure that you pray daily. Given that recommendation, you may wonder how to put it into practice. Feel free to modify this to suit your needs, but here's what I suggest for starters.

Set aside a regular time and place to pray—I have found this to be critical. You can either create a new place (a home altar or chapel) or use an existing place (your car, an office, outdoors, a church). Over time this place will become special, because that's where you and the Lord converse. I do some of my best praying in the car or at my desk. Choose a place that works for you, and stick to it.

Writing down your prayers is an excellent way to remain focused and helps the Lord become real to you. When I first heard this suggestion, I thought it was silly. The more I thought about it, however, the more I felt compelled to give it a try. I'm glad that I did, because it has helped me tremendously. I generally limit myself to one page, but sometimes I'll write more. I recommend that you get a notebook in which you can write a letter to Jesus every day. You can assess your spiritual progress by looking back through previous entries.

During your daily prayer time, speak, ask questions, and listen. If you're not used to speaking with the Lord, don't get too hung up on the words. Treat him as a friend, because that's exactly who he is. Share your thoughts, fears, and confusion with him. Tell him you love him, and ask him to reveal himself to you. Ask him what you can do for him. Praise him for his greatness, and thank him for his blessings. Beg for the graces that you need in order to remain holy and to make it through the day.

If you're confused about something in your life, don't hesitate to ask Jesus about it. Then be patient and wait for an answer. He can answer you in many ways—through the Bible, with a feeling of peace or a thought, through a friend, or even through nature. Sometimes he uses the circumstances of our lives to speak to us. These are not always comfortable: You may be turned down for a job or denied admission to a certain college. But these happenings might point the way to something else. Sometimes God's answer to our dilemmas is "Just trust me."

Use some of your prayer time to pray for your family, friends, the poor, the suffering, those who are not close to the Lord, and the souls in purgatory. Be sure to pray for your own needs (material and spiritual) as well.

You might struggle with prayer in the beginning, but it gets easier with time. The *Catechism* reminds us that the Holy Spirit can teach us to pray, especially through the Sacred Tradition (see CCC 2650) of the Church. Besides using your own words to pray, you might also like to incorporate some formal prayers into your daily routine. That's something that I do. The Church offers many of these prayers, so which ones should you use?

When one of his disciples asked Jesus how to pray, he responded with the following words:

> Our Father who art in heaven,
> Hallowed be thy name.
> Thy kingdom come.
> Thy will be done,
> On earth as it is in heaven.
> Give us this day our daily bread;
> And forgive us our trespasses,
> As we forgive those who trespass against us.
> And lead us not into temptation,
> But deliver us from evil. (Matthew 6:9–13)

Amen. Any prayer that Jesus recommends is probably a good one to pray every day!

Don't Forget...

1. The Church recognizes that there are several different forms of prayer, and it's a good idea to use them all.
2. Prayers of blessing and adoration recognize God's goodness to us.
3. We offer prayers of intercession when we ask the Lord for favors on behalf of others.
4. In order to pray, "one must have the will to pray" (CCC 2650).

5. When asked how to pray, Jesus responded by giving us the Our Father or Lord's Prayer.

JESUS SAYS...

"And I tell you, Ask, and it will be given you; seek, and you will find; knock, and it will be opened to you." (Luke 11:9)

# step four Listen!

◦ ◦ ◦

All Scripture is inspired by God and profitable for teaching,
for reproof, for correction, and for training in righteousness,
that the man of God may be complete, equipped
for every good work.
—2 Timothy 3:16–17

God never speaks to me." Does this sound familiar? As I travel around the country sharing the Good News, I hear this statement repeatedly. And it's completely untrue.

The Lord speaks in several ways, the most reliable of which is the Bible. If you read the Bible or even listen to the readings at Mass, he is speaking to you. Here's what the Church says: "For in the sacred books, the Father who is in heaven meets His children with great love and speaks with them" (*Dei Verbum*, 21).

You and I have the opportunity to hear the Lord's voice several times each day. All we have to do is open up our Bibles. That's very impressive, isn't it? It's often difficult to get a live person on the telephone when we need customer support, but we can hear the Lord's voice whenever we want simply by reading Sacred Scripture.

While it's definitely a great deal, it can be a struggle to get used to listening in this manner. As a cradle Catholic, I was not used to reading the Bible. My parents made sure that we went to Mass every Sunday, but reading Scripture was not something that was practiced in the Zimak household.

That's not to say that we didn't have a Bible. We had a beautiful family Bible that was given to us by a priest friend. It had a padded cover with a picture of Jesus on it. Just looking at it, one could tell that it was a special book. It was such a treasured possession, in fact, that it remained in the closet (in a sturdy cardboard box) for safekeeping. We treated the written Word of God as a valued keepsake. As a result, we failed to hear the Lord speak to us.

I now know that this is a very common story. Many Catholics treated (or continue to treat) the Bible in the same way. This is unfortunate, because reading the Bible is a great way to encounter Christ. If you want to hear him speak, you'll want to incorporate some Scripture reading into your daily routine.

UNDERSTANDING SCRIPTURE

Don't be fooled if someone tells you that the Bible is an easy read. St. Peter tells us just the opposite in a message contained in, of all places, the Bible! Referring first to the letters of St. Paul and then to the rest of Scripture, he states: "There are some things in them hard to understand, which the ignorant and unstable twist to their own destruction, as they do the other Scriptures" (2 Peter 3:16).

It may seem odd that I'm beginning a section on the importance of the Bible with the news that it can be difficult to read, but there really is a method to my madness. First, if people tell you (and some will) that the Bible is easy to understand, you're going to be in for a surprise when you open it up. And if you're like me, you might become discouraged and think that you're not smart enough to understand it. As a result, you'll probably stop reading it in a very short period of time.

Second, ignoring the complexity of Sacred Scripture can cause you to misinterpret the Lord's message, thus falling into the trap St. Peter refers to above. God gives us a solution, one that we find right in Scripture.

In the Acts of the Apostles, Philip (one of the first deacons) encountered an Ethiopian official on the road from Jerusalem to Gaza (see Acts 8:26–40). The man was seated in his chariot, reading the book of the prophet Isaiah. Prompted by the Holy Spirit, Philip asked the man if he understood what he was reading. His answer? "How can I, unless some one guides me?" (Acts 8:31).

We're told that the Ethiopian was reading Isaiah 53:7–8 and was confused about whether it referred to the prophet or to someone else. Philip pointed out that it was a reference to Jesus, and he ended up baptizing the man.

Aside from being a great example of how to evangelize, this incident illustrates the importance of seeking guidance when reading the Bible. Furthermore, the fact that Philip was a deacon (an ordained minister of the Church) provides an excellent lead-in to my next point. The guidance that we need in order to hear the Lord's voice in Sacred Scripture (without misunderstanding his message) comes from the Church.

While we are free (and encouraged) to read the Bible frequently and apply God's message to our lives, the Church is the ultimate guardian of Sacred Scripture. Here is the official position, as stated in the Vatican II document *Dei Verbum*:

> But, since Holy Scripture must be read and interpreted in the sacred spirit in which it was written, no less serious attention must be given to the content and unity of the whole of Scripture if the meaning of the sacred texts is to be correctly worked out. The living tradition of the whole Church must be taken into account along with the harmony which exists between elements of the faith. It is the task of exegetes to work according to these rules toward a better understanding and explanation of the meaning of Sacred Scripture, so that through preparatory study the judgment of the Church may mature. For all of what has been said about the way of interpreting Scripture is subject finally to the judgment of the Church, which carries out the divine commission and ministry of guarding and interpreting the word of God. (*Dei Verbum*, 12)

While the Church doesn't give a verse-by-verse interpretation of the Bible, we should always keep Catholic teaching in mind when we read Scripture. And we should never interpret Scripture in a way that contradicts a teaching of the Church. At first this may seem restrictive, but it's actually very comforting. If God really does speak to me through the Bible, shouldn't I want to ensure that I'm hearing him correctly? The Catholic Church compiled the books of the Bible (deciding which ones are inspired by God), so it only makes sense that she should protect us from incorrectly hearing the Lord's message.

If I ignore Church teaching when reading the Bible, my interpretation could very well be incorrect. If I read the Bible and conclude that God is telling me that it's acceptable to practice birth control, skip Mass on Sunday, or obtain an abortion, I'm not hearing him correctly. People have been doing this kind of thing for years. That is one of the reasons there are so many Christian denominations. The Church existed before the Bible. Always read Scripture with your Catholic goggles firmly in place!

With that in mind, how can I open my Bible and enter into a relationship with the Lord? Do I just start at the beginning, should I open up to a random page, or is it a good idea to look at my favorite verses? Furthermore, how can I hear God speaking to me when I'm reading his Word?

WHERE TO START

Let's tackle the "where to start" question first. Whether you're a Scripture scholar or a complete Bible beginner, I recommend that you incorporate the daily Mass readings, taken directly from the Bible, into your spiritual reading. This is a great way to let the Church guide you through the Scriptures, and it only takes a few minutes a day. You can find the readings online at the United States Catholic Bishops website (www.usccb.org) and in magazines such as *The Word Among Us* (www.wau.org) and *Magnificat* (www.magnificat.com). In addition, you can use a daily missal, such as the excellent *Daily Roman Missal* published by Midwest Theological Forum (www.theological-forum.org). I use a combination of these resources each day, and they are great ways to journey through the Bible.

This practice will help you develop an understanding of how the Old and New Testaments fit together. By reading the Responsorial Psalm for daily Mass, you can often see the common theme that ties the readings together.

Reading the Bible in this manner can also help us avoid the habit of just reading what we want to read. While it's a good idea to become familiar with certain Bible verses (I have my favorites), we can sometimes limit ourselves by constantly reading the same message. Using the daily Mass readings helps us remain open to what God wants us to hear for that day. Quite often, it's not the message we want to hear but the one we need to hear!

Another recommended way to read the Bible (which works equally well for beginners and experts) is to give special attention to the Gospels. The Church recognizes that "the Gospels have a special preeminence" (*Dei Verbum*, 18) among the Scriptures, as they tell the story of Jesus Christ. Reading Christ's story is an excellent way to grow closer to him.

Over the years, I have heard many differing recommendations about which Gospel should be read first. Personally, I believe that the Gospel of Mark is a good place to start. It is the shortest of the four and focuses on the great works performed by the Lord. After that I would read Luke, Matthew, and John in that order, but that's just my personal preference. What's important is that you choose an approach that you can stick with.

Finally, when reading the Gospels, don't try to read too much at once. One chapter a day should be sufficient. If you have a tendency to speed read (as I do!), you could easily miss some important details. Relax and take your time. By doing so, you'll be amazed at what you hear!

Now that we've looked at what to read, let's spend the rest of this section discussing a technique that will turn your reading into an encounter with the Lord.

## LECTIO DIVINA

Instead of reading Scripture as you would any other book, you can turn Bible reading into a dialogue with the Lord. The ancient practice known as *lectio divina* (Latin for "sacred reading") makes this possible. And despite the fancy name and hard-to-believe promise, the basic concept is really quite simple. Are you ready to have a meaningful conversation with the Lord by using the Bible?

Let's break it down into a set of steps. In order to make it easier to understand the process, I'll use one of my favorite Gospel passages. It is the familiar story of Peter walking on the water, with a big assist from Christ (see Matthew 14:22–33).

Just prior to this passage, Jesus approached the disciples, who were in a boat that was being "beaten by the waves." Jesus was walking on the water. The disciples were terrified and thought that he was a ghost. Jesus spoke to them and said, "Take heart, it is I; have no fear."

Now it was Peter's turn to speak:

> And Peter answered him, "Lord, if it is you, bid me come to you on the water." He said, "Come." So Peter got out of the boat and walked on the water and came to Jesus; but when he saw the wind, he was afraid, and beginning to sink he cried out, "Lord, save me." Jesus immediately reached out his hand and caught him, saying to him, "O you of little faith, why did you doubt?" And when they got into the boat, the wind ceased. And those in the boat worshiped him, saying, "Truly you are the Son of God." (Matthew 14:28–33)

• *What Does It Say?*

The first step in *lectio divina* is to simply read the story and process the details. All we are doing here is looking at the facts: what happened and who was involved.

In the above passage, Peter responded to Jesus and requested an invitation to walk on the water. Upon receiving that invitation, he exited the boat and walked on the water toward Jesus. Seeing the wind, however, Peter began to sink. He then cried out to the Lord, who after questioning his faith, delivered him safely to the boat. At that point, with Jesus in the boat, the wind ceased. Those in the boat worshiped him and recognized his role as the Son of God.

• *What Does It Say to Me?*

Many people tend to treat the stories in the Bible as nothing more than history lessons. That is a mistake. The Lord speaks to us in the Bible. Our next step is to consider what he is saying to us personally.

Here's what the Lord told me the last time I read this passage:

> Gary, I'm calling you to trust me with the uncertainties of your life. Even though you have many fears and concerns, I am with you. I won't promise that you'll never have problems, but I do promise that I'll always be with you. I'm not going to force you, however. The choice is yours to make. Do you trust me enough to get out of the boat and walk on the water?

Jesus's message to you could be much different; and his message to me can differ each time I read this passage. "For the word of God is living and active, sharper than any two-edged sword, piercing to the division of soul and spirit, of joints and marrow, and discerning the thoughts and intentions of the heart" (Hebrews 4:12).

• *What Do I Want to Say to the Lord?*
After listening to the Lord speak to me through this passage, it's my turn to respond to him. My response might sound something like this:

> I want to trust you, Lord, but I'm afraid. If you really want me to leave my comfort zone and come to you, let me know. Let me hear your voice in the Bible and in the silence of my heart when I pray. Help me to trust you with my life. It's not easy for me, because I'm so weak. I'm afraid that I might make a mistake. I know that you can always bring good out of any situation, but sometimes I forget when the storms of life beat me down. You saved Peter when he began to sink, and I know you can save me too. Please help me to trust you, Lord. I really want to walk on the water and be with you!

REST IN HIS PRESENCE
Now it's time to be silent and rest in the Lord's presence. Unlike what happens when I read an ordinary book, I just had a personal encounter with the author of the Bible. I need to reflect on what just happened. I need to spend some time enjoying the security of his presence.

When I was a child, my mother worked at night. Even though my father was home with my sister and me, something was missing when Mom wasn't there. On those days when both of my parents were home in the evening, I felt more secure. My mother's presence made me feel better. That's kind of the sense the Lord gives me when I read and meditate on his Word.

• *Live It!*

Now that we've completed the reading and meditation, it's time to put what we have learned into practice. In the case of the above passage, there's a good chance we'll be given the opportunity rather quickly. Every day, we are presented with challenging situations that require trust. Am I willing to trust in God's providence? How will I react when I begin to sink? I'll never know until I get out into the sea of this world and give it a try.

That's what this final step in the process is all about. Sometimes we'll succeed, and sometimes we'll fail, but what really matters is that we try. If it doesn't work out well, there's always tomorrow. Keep trying to meet the Lord in the Bible and live the message in your daily life!

Applying these steps to my Scripture reading has helped me tremendously, and I know that it will do the same for you. You will have to work at it, but you'll never regret the effort.

Every day, you and I have the opportunity to enter into conversation with the Lord. The Bible is a very reliable way of making that encounter possible. Don't make the mistake of overlooking this great gift.

When you read Scripture daily, your life will change. I didn't believe it until I started putting it into practice. Give it a try, and see what happens.

DON'T FORGET...

1. The Bible is a very reliable way of hearing the Lord's voice.

2. We should never try to interpret the Bible without considering the Church's teaching.

3. Every time we read Sacred Scripture, we have an encounter with the Lord.

4. If we want to have a close, personal relationship with Jesus, we must read the Bible daily.

5. Through the ancient practice known as *lectio divina*, we can converse with the Lord through our Scripture reading.

JESUS SAYS…

"My sheep hear my voice, and I know them, and they follow me." (John 10:27)

## step five **Go for the Grace**

◦ ◦ ◦

By grace you have been saved through faith; and this is not your own doing, it is the gift of God—not because of works, lest any man should boast.

—EPHESIANS 2:8–9

When I first started to think about writing this book, I was actively looking for ideas. Having a personal relationship with Jesus is so important that I didn't want to leave out any steps. While searching the Internet one day, something caught my attention in a big way.

In a homily on May 16, 2014, Pope Francis offered advice for getting to know Jesus. He discussed prayer, which came as no surprise, but I was very much surprised by his next piece of advice:

> Prayer on its own is not enough, we need the joy of cele-
> bration. We must celebrate Jesus through his Sacraments,
> because these give us life, they give us strength, they nourish
> us, they comfort us, they forge an alliance with us, they
> give us a mission. Without celebrating the Sacraments,
> we'll never get to know Jesus.[8]

Please understand that I am a cradle Catholic, and I thought that I was familiar with the sacraments. I knew that Jesus was fully present in the Eucharist, but the thought of encountering him in the other sacraments was foreign to me. Do we really meet Jesus in each of the seven sacraments?

After doing some research, I discovered that the Church teaches that we do. This fact is stated clearly in the *Catechism*:

> Celebrated worthily in faith, the sacraments confer the grace that they signify. They are *efficacious* because in them Christ himself is at work: it is he who baptizes, he who acts in his sacraments in order to communicate the grace that each sacrament signifies. (CCC 1127)

This concept is truly mind-boggling. If Jesus is working in the sacraments, then I meet him every time I receive any one of them. When I was baptized, it was Jesus who wiped away my original sin and welcomed me into his Church. When I was confirmed, it was Jesus who increased the gifts of the Holy Spirit and gave me the strength to defend the Catholic faith and become a witness to those around me. Every time I go to confession, it is Christ himself who forgives me for my sins. Whenever I receive Holy Communion, it is Jesus who gives himself to me in the most intimate way imaginable. Wow!

Why wasn't this clear to me in the past? How did I miss it? Furthermore, why didn't I hear other Catholics discussing it?

## SACRAMENTAL ENCOUNTERS

It's sad that many people fail to make the connection between the sacraments and a relationship with Jesus. And in all fairness, it's not really their fault. There are several reasons why it can be difficult to see the sacraments as encounters with Christ.

First of all, Jesus is now invisible and works through his Church. When I receive the sacraments, I can't actually see Jesus. All I see is an encounter with a member of the clergy. Even though the Lord is present and very much involved, my senses don't tell me that.

Second, the sacraments are often treated as important milestones in our lives, celebrated with big parties. While this isn't a bad thing, the visible celebrations can cause us to lose sight of the sacraments' invisible effects (and the presence of Jesus). I don't know about you, but when I was confirmed, my focus was on gifts and food, and not on the fact that I was now equipped to defend my Catholic faith. The same thing happens at many weddings: The reception is appreciated more than the sacramental union that takes place in the church.

But is it really a problem if we don't understand the inner workings of the sacraments? Don't they still work even if we don't understand all of the details? Yes and no. Here is what the Church teaches:

> [The Church affirms] that the sacraments act *ex opere operato* (literally: "by the very fact of the action's being performed"), i.e., by virtue of the saving work of Christ, accomplished once for all. It follows that "the sacrament is not wrought by the righteousness of either the celebrant or the recipient, but by the power of God." From the moment that a sacrament is celebrated in accordance with the intention of the Church, the power of Christ and his Spirit acts in and through it, independently of the personal holiness of the minister. Nevertheless, the fruits of the sacraments also depend on the disposition of the one who

receives them. (CCC 1128; see Council of Trent: DS 1608; quote is from St. Thomas Aquinas, *Summa Theologiae* III, 68, 8)

The effectiveness of the sacraments is not dependent upon the holiness of the minister or the recipient. Each of the sacraments will produce the intended grace, as desired by Christ. However, and this is a big *however*, it is not a given that the grace will bear the same amount of fruit in each of us. In other words, our intent really does matter.

> The sacraments are efficacious signs of grace, instituted by Christ and entrusted to the Church, by which divine life is dispensed to us. The visible rites by which the sacraments are celebrated signify and make present the graces proper to each sacrament. They bear fruit in those who receive them with the required dispositions. (CCC 1131)

Even though I was baptized and confirmed and received Holy Communion weekly, I spent many years as a lukewarm Catholic. I didn't care about the Lord or his Church. Essentially, I was going through the motions. There's no doubt that I received a great deal of grace over the years, but my apathetic disposition blocked it from bearing fruit in my life. I had numerous encounters with Jesus but did not allow those to spark a deep relationship with him.

Pope St. John Paul II recognized this problem in his apostolic exhortation *Catechesi Tradendae* (On Catechesis in Our Time):

> A certain number of children baptized in infancy come for catechesis in the parish without receiving any other

initiation into the faith and still without any explicit personal attachment to Jesus Christ; they only have the capacity to believe placed within them by Baptism and the presence of the Holy Spirit. (*Catechesi Tradendae*, 19)[9]

As I have personally experienced, the fact that we receive the sacraments doesn't ensure that we will have a personal relationship with Jesus Christ. Even though tons of graces are flowing our way, we could unintentionally block them from bearing fruit in our lives. Pretty frightening, isn't it?

There is good news: This problem is completely fixable, and the fix is totally within our control. The only thing stopping the sacraments from drawing us closer to Jesus and bearing great fruit in our lives is—you guessed it—us!

What can we do about this dilemma? How do we ensure that we don't waste the great gifts given to us by the Lord?

In short, we have to care. When we receive the sacraments, we should have a desire to grow closer to the Lord and to receive the grace that is available. If you're concerned that you don't have that desire, ask for it.

Jesus knows that we are distracted by the events of daily life. He understands that we often lose sight of spiritual treasures and become preoccupied with material things. That's why he wants us to ask for help.

If you're reading this book, you obviously have a desire to grow closer to the Lord. Therefore, you're on the right track. Ask him for an increased desire to encounter him in the sacraments. It might not happen overnight, but you'll be amazed at what he can do.

APPRECIATING THE EUCHARIST

While Jesus is present in all of the sacraments, let's use the remainder of this section to focus on meeting him in the Eucharist. How important is this sacrament?

> The Eucharist is "the source and summit of the Christian life." "The other sacraments, and indeed all ecclesiastical ministries and works of the apostolate, are bound up with the Eucharist and are oriented toward it. For in the blessed Eucharist is contained the whole spiritual good of the Church, namely Christ himself, our Pasch." (CCC 1324, quoting *Lumen Gentium*, 11; *Presbyterorum Ordinis*, 5)

We often fail to appreciate the Lord's real presence when we receive him in Holy Communion. Even though the Eucharist is an intimate, personal encounter with the same Jesus that we read about in the Gospels, we can easily become distracted. As a result, our desire isn't what it should be, and we miss out on the full effect of the Sacrament.

Fortunately, there are some simple steps that we can take to better appreciate the gift of Our Lord in the Eucharist.

• *Ask for Help*

We have already touched on this, but it's important enough to discuss in greater depth. As humans, we have a tendency to trust our senses to perceive the world. "Seeing is believing" is more than just a saying. It's difficult to appreciate an encounter with an unseen Jesus that provides us with invisible grace. Feeling this way doesn't make you a bad person; it makes you human.

It is also difficult to value spiritual gifts over material gifts. If every reception of Holy Communion resulted in a one-hundred-dollar rebate, daily Mass attendance would go through the roof! There are many times when we don't feel any different after receiving the Eucharist. A subconscious message to our brain indicates that the Sacrament has no effect.

With all of these factors working against us, it's no wonder that our desire to receive the Sacrament isn't as strong as it could be. Don't make the mistake of trying to force yourself to care. Instead, take the counterintuitive approach of asking the Lord for help.

Asking for help may feel strange. It might make you feel less than honorable, but it's the first thing you should do. If you want a stronger desire to encounter Jesus in the Eucharist, ask him to give you that desire. He won't let you down. Your appreciation for this great sacrament will increase over time. Just make sure that you keep asking for help!

"No one can come to me unless the Father who sent me draws him" (John 6:44).

• *Think About It*

Please excuse my bluntness with what I'm about to say, but it's something that needs to be said. Unless we spend time thinking about the Lord's miraculous and generous presence in the Eucharist, we're never going to care as much as we should.

In his book *Healed Through Cancer and Other Adversities* (Tate, 2012), my friend Jim Littleton told of how his battle with an aggressive form of leukemia drew him closer to the Lord. The story is a powerful one of God's help in the midst of great struggles, and the message was magnified for me when I learned one important fact: Jim wrote much of the book from a hospital bed, dictating the words to his daughters while facing a completely uncertain future. Although he is cancer-free as of this writing, that was certainly not the case when he was working on the book.

Learning the backstory made the book really hit home with me. I was blown away by the fact that Jim believed so strongly in his message that he took extraordinary steps to ensure that it was transmitted. This made me appreciate what he was saying that much more.

In a similar way, Christ was prepared to do whatever was necessary to remain with us even after he ascended into heaven. He was even willing to humble himself and appear under the appearance of ordinary bread and wine. Meditating on his humility and desire to be with us is a sure way to increase our desire for this great sacrament. When we receive Holy Communion, it may look like bread, but it isn't. We are receiving Jesus! In addition, we are also receiving the grace to become holy and deal with the struggles of daily life.

I invite you to spend some time thinking about this before your next Communion. Jesus loves you so much that he miraculously makes it possible for you to consume his very Body, Blood, soul, and divinity. What an awesome gift!

• *Imagine It's Your Last*

Did you ever take a memorable trip? Do you remember how you felt on the final day? If you're like me, you probably tried very hard to appreciate your surroundings before you returned home. You wanted to make the experience last, right?

Now, think back to the last time you received Jesus in Holy Communion. Even though it may seem improbable, there is no guarantee that you will ever have the chance to receive him again. With that in mind, how would you have reacted if it was truly the last time you'd ever receive him in this life? Would you have thanked him more? Would you have begged to receive all possible graces? Would you have asked him to help you with your problems? Would you have savored being intimately united with your Lord and Savior?

The next time you receive Jesus in the Eucharist, treat it as if it's the last time you'll ever receive him. You will be amazed at how your appreciation for him will grow.

This book is all about becoming closer to Jesus. If you're reading it, you obviously have that desire. While all of the sacraments allow us to encounter Christ, Holy Communion takes that encounter to a whole new level. The practice of daily Communion has transformed my relationship with Jesus into an intimate friendship. Although I will continue to work on our relationship for the rest of my life, I can definitely say that we have become good friends.

If you have the chance, I strongly encourage you to attend daily Mass and receive Jesus as often as possible. It is by far the most important advice that I can give you. "*Holy Communion augments our union with Christ.* The principal fruit of receiving the Eucharist in Holy Communion is an intimate union with Christ Jesus" (*CCC* 1391).

DON'T FORGET...

1. We encounter Jesus whenever we receive any of the sacraments.

2. The effectiveness of the sacraments depends on our disposition when we receive them.

3. The Eucharist is the "source and summit" of the Christian life.

4. We can't just force ourselves to better appreciate the Eucharist. We should ask the Lord to help us.

5. Holy Communion is the most effective means of uniting ourselves with Jesus.

Jesus Says...

"For my flesh is food indeed, and my blood is drink indeed. He who eats my flesh and drinks my blood abides in me, and I in him." (John 6:55–56)

## step six Enjoy His Real Presence

❖ ❖ ❖

My soul is very sorrowful, even to death; remain here, and
watch with me.

—MATTHEW 26:38

In order to share the Good News with people all over the
United States and Canada, travel is a necessity. Although I
love being a full-time speaker and author, I don't enjoy being
away from my family. Fortunately, I can communicate with my
wife and daughters by phone, e-mail, and social media. I have
called Eileen many times from airports and hotels, and it's great
to hear the sound of her voice. At times, it feels as if she is right
there with me.

As good as it is to be able to chat in this way, nothing beats
walking through the front door and getting big hugs from Eileen
and my daughters, Mary and Elizabeth. It's just great being with
people you love.

We are blessed to be able to speak with Jesus from any place
at any time. I speak to him in the car, while I'm lying in bed at
night, and even in the shower. While these spiritual encounters
are very comforting, there is one encounter that is even more
comforting—being with Jesus in the Eucharist.

Even when I look back on my days as a lukewarm Catholic, I remember the peaceful feeling that I would get when I walked into a church. I didn't appreciate it at the time, but I was able to feel the Lord's presence in the tabernacle. And I have come to realize that my story is not unique; I have met many individuals who have experienced the same phenomenon. Conversely, if you have ever entered a Catholic church on Good Friday or Holy Saturday (when Jesus is not in the tabernacle), you know how empty it feels. When the Lord is absent, you can feel it.

### Saints and the Eucharist

Why is it important to spend time in the presence of Jesus? Before I share my own personal experience, here are the thoughts of two spiritual giants.

> It is pleasant to spend time with him, to lie close to his breast like the Beloved Disciple (see John 13:25) and to feel the infinite love present in his heart. If in our time Christians must be distinguished above all by the "art of prayer," how can we not feel a renewed need to spend time in spiritual converse, in silent adoration, in heartfelt love before Christ present in the Most Holy Sacrament? How often, dear brother and sisters, have I experienced this, and drawn from it strength, consolation and support![10]

It's apparent from reading St. John Paul II's words that he had a close, personal relationship with the Lord. I love that image of lying close to Jesus's breast. Note that the pope also feels the infinite love present on the Lord's heart.

Some of you may look at the Holy Father's statement and think that it's not possible for you to get to this level of intimacy with the Lord. Although it takes time to get there, it is totally possible. How can you do it? Spending time with him is a great place to start.

Archbishop Fulton Sheen made no secret about his love for spending time with the Lord in Eucharistic Adoration. On the day of his ordination, he vowed to make a holy hour before the Blessed Sacrament every day of his life. It was a promise that he kept. In his autobiography, Sheen explains some of the reasons why he remained faithful to that vow and why he recommends it to others:

> As Paul puts it: "We are transfigured into His likeness, from splendor to splendor." We become like that which we gaze upon. Looking into a sunset, the face takes on a golden glow. Looking at the Eucharistic Lord for an hour transforms the heart in a mysterious way as the face of Moses was transformed after his companionship with God on the mountain. Something happens to us similar to that which happened to the disciples at Emmaus. On Easter Sunday afternoon when the Lord met them, He asked why they were so gloomy. After spending some time in His presence, and hearing again the secret of spirituality—"The Son of Man must suffer to enter into His Glory"—their time with him ended and their "hearts were on fire.".…
>
> The purpose of the Holy Hour is to encourage deep personal encounter with Christ. The holy and glorious God is constantly inviting us to come to Him, to hold converse with Him, to ask for such things as we need and to experience what a blessing there is in fellowship with Him.[11]

## MY STORY

If you want to grow closer to Jesus, spending time with him is essential. And in case you're curious, I can personally vouch for the accuracy of that statement.

It took me many years to make Eucharistic Adoration a regular practice in my life. In all honesty, I just didn't get it. Even though I felt that sense of peace whenever I walked into a Catholic church, I didn't realize that what I was feeling was the real presence of Christ.

So what happened? What caused me to begin spending time before the Blessed Sacrament on a regular basis?

I was first introduced to the idea of Eucharistic Adoration by a priest in the early eighties, but it seemed like too much work. Sitting there quietly in the presence of the white host was, to be completely honest, painful. Even though I knew that it was Jesus (and not a piece of bread), I just couldn't appreciate the value of being there and doing seemingly nothing for an entire hour.

Eventually two people came into my life who had a great influence on how I would view Adoration. By their actions and devotion, my wife and her mother helped me to appreciate the importance of spending time with Jesus in this special way.

When Eileen and I started dating in 1993, we often spent time in the Adoration chapel. Eileen made a regular holy hour each week, and I would frequently accompany her. Although I struggled at times, the thought of being in the presence of Jesus with someone I loved was very appealing to me.

After we got married, Eileen and I continued to spend an hour each week with the Lord. As the weeks passed, I started to appreciate that hour more and more. Jesus's presence became a great source of comfort to me, especially as we dealt with infertility. Each week, we would retreat from a world that made no promises and spend time with Jesus, who promised that all things are possible.

Eileen became pregnant with our twin daughters, Mary and Elizabeth, in 1997. Shortly after receiving the good news, however, we were told that the girls were suffering from an often fatal condition known as twin-to-twin transfusion syndrome. The news prompted us to pray very hard for the next few months, which included many visits to the Adoration chapel. Being with the Lord during this difficult time was very comforting to us.

Fortunately, the girls defied the odds and lived, entering the world three months early. This was a wonderful thing, a real answer to prayer. But the chaos brought on by having premature twins caused us to give up our regular hour before the Lord. It would be several years before I was able to get back on track.

Eileen's mother, Betty Moynahan, loved Jesus and spent many hours praying before him in the Blessed Sacrament. She would talk about him frequently, and I would sometimes envy their relationship. If only I hadn't been so busy. I had young children who still had some health issues, I had a job, and I had family responsibilities. I probably should have gone to be with Jesus, but I just didn't have the time.

BACK TO THE CHAPEL

In late 2004, however, I received a major wake-up call. After experiencing strange symptoms (weight loss, nausea, mysterious pain in the side) for several weeks, I went to see my doctor. A series of diagnostic tests revealed that I had enlarged lymph nodes in my abdomen. I was sent to a hematologist, who speculated that I might be suffering from low-grade lymphoma. I didn't know a lot about the disease, but I knew that it was serious. Over the next several months, the doctors took a wait-and-see approach, monitoring my condition closely. The lymph nodes continued to grow, which ruled out a simple virus as the probable cause.

Guess who found his way back to the Adoration chapel? I then made it a point to stop by the chapel before and after work every day. Isn't it amazing how I was suddenly able to make time for Jesus as soon as I thought I was dying?

In time, the symptoms vanished, and the lymph nodes went back to their normal size. No official diagnosis was ever made. Coincidence? I don't think so. This incident not only caused me to get back to spending time with Jesus in Adoration but was the driving force behind my conversion from lukewarm Catholic to Catholic on fire.

Now that I spend some time before the Eucharist every day, let me share with you how it has changed my life. For one thing, I have lost count of how many times I've received solutions to my problems while sitting before Jesus in the Adoration chapel. What's unusual about this is that these answers typically pop into my head. There have been numerous occasions when I was completely baffled about a problem that I was facing, only to sit in the chapel and suddenly think of a potential solution. I could possibly write these off as coincidences if they didn't occur so often.

In addition, I feel a great sense of peace when I'm with the Lord. It's similar to the feeling that I get when I wake up in the night and see my wife asleep next to me. Even though Eileen isn't saying anything, I feel a sense of comfort just knowing that she's there. When I'm in the chapel with Jesus, I can absolutely feel his presence. All of my books (including this one) have been written (at least in part) while sitting before Jesus.

As I mentioned, however, I didn't always feel this way. When I first started spending time with the Lord in Adoration, I would constantly fidget and look at my watch. Even though I knew that it was important to be there, I sometimes felt like crawling out of my skin. Just sitting there in silence would drive me crazy. So how was I able to overcome this discomfort?

I can't take the credit for it. All I did was keep showing up. It was the Lord who made it happen. Each time I was there, Jesus reached out to me, and eventually we became close friends.

Once we decide to become friends with Christ, we might make the mistake of trying to do all the work. We can lose sight of the fact that he's also working on the relationship. As we're reaching out to him and spending time in his presence, he's also sharing himself with us. As we continue to do this, we eventually become more comfortable hanging out with him.

I can honestly say that I'm now sorry when it's time to leave the chapel. When I'm in the real presence of Christ, it's a little bit of heaven on earth!

### What Do I Do?

Before I bring this section to a close, I want to address the most common question that I hear about Eucharistic Adoration: What should I do while I'm there? Should I kneel or sit? Should I read, or is it better to pray? If I pray, what should I say?

These are all very good questions, but more important than what you say or do is the fact that you're there. You are keeping the Lord company, and there's no need to panic about what you say or do. Even if you fall asleep in the Lord's presence, it's not the first time that he's seen it. Just ask St. Peter, St. James, and St. John!

With that in mind, here is what I would recommend if you're new to Eucharistic Adoration. Although a desirable goal would be to spend an hour with the Lord, start out by going for fifteen minutes. I fear that if you start with an hour, it will seem overwhelming, and you might not want to come back. On the other hand, fifteen minutes is very doable.

Once you enter into the Lord's presence, say hello (you don't have to say it audibly) and tell him that you're here to keep him company. Thank him for all of the blessings in your life. Share with him any problems or concerns that you may have, and ask him to handle them for you. You can also mention any family members or friends who have asked for your prayers. Before you leave, ask Jesus to increase your desire to be with him. Then make the decision to return the following week.

When you feel ready, increase your time in the chapel to thirty minutes, forty-five minutes, an hour. Don't be in a hurry to do this, however. Let it happen naturally.

Once you are comfortable spending time with the Lord, devote a portion of your visit to listening to him speak. How is that done? As we discussed in step 4, the easiest and most accurate method of hearing the Lord (especially if you're a beginner) is to open up the Bible. Here are some verses that I'd recommend to get you started:

> "Come to me, all who labor and are heavy laden, and I will give you rest." (Matthew 11:28)

"Follow me." (Matthew 9:9)

"Take heart, it is I; have no fear." (Matthew 14:27)

"With men this is impossible, but with God all things are possible." (Matthew 19:26)

"Why are you afraid? Have you no faith?" (Mark 4:40)

"I am the light of the world; he who follows me will not walk in darkness, but will have the light of life." (John 8:12)

"If you love me, you will keep my commandments." (John 14:15)

"Peace be with you." (John 20:19)

You could also slowly read one of the Gospels and pause whenever a certain verse gets your attention.

The important thing to remember is that the Lord speaks to you every time you open the Bible. Although he also speaks in other ways, this is the most foolproof way of hearing his voice. It's even more special when you do it in his presence.

As you become more comfortable spending time with Jesus, you will hear him speak to you in other ways. Ask him if he has anything to say to you, and then listen. That's right, just listen! His message may come in the form of a thought or a feeling. You might recall something said by a friend or as part of a homily from Mass. Or you may just experience a feeling of peace.

If your mind drifts, don't beat yourself up over it. My spiritual director advised me to bring those distracting thoughts to prayer. If you're thinking about a person or situation, there might be a reason. Instead of worrying about it, ask the Lord to help you.

Eventually, as you and Jesus get to know each other better, it will feel natural to be in his presence. Even if you're having a bad day and don't have much to say, you'll enjoy spending time with him. We've all heard the familiar saying "Absence makes the heart grow fonder," but with the Lord, it's simply not true. Absence from Jesus will never make you love him more. Being in his presence will!

DON'T FORGET...

1. Spending time in the presence of Jesus is a great way to get to know him better.

2. According to Archbishop Fulton Sheen, the purpose of the holy hour is to encourage a deep, personal encounter with Christ.

3. When first beginning to pray before Jesus in the Blessed Sacrament, start with about fifteen minutes. You can increase the time as you become more comfortable.

4. Reading the Bible (especially in the presence of Jesus) is a great way to hear him speak.

5. Time spent with the Lord in adoration is never wasted. Many graces flow from it.

JESUS SAYS...

"So, could you not watch with me one hour?" (Matthew 26:40)

✳ ❧ ❀

Do whatever he tells you.

—JOHN 2:5

My family and I always enjoy taking a ride to Cape May, New Jersey. Whenever we visit, one of the first things we do is stop by Our Lady Star of the Sea Church. Just over the main entrance is an image of the Blessed Mother and the words *Ad Jesum Per Mariam* (Latin for "To Jesus through Mary").

I have to admit that I was confused when I first learned the meaning of these words. I wondered how Mary could help me get to Jesus. Furthermore, any time I spend talking to the Blessed Mother is time that I don't spend talking with Jesus, so how could this message be true?

Questions like this can lead us to a greater understanding and an increased faith. Even though it may not seem like it, our questions (or even doubts) are often the result of Christ's reaching out to us. Provided we remain open minded, seeking answers is a great way to grow in faith.

As a cradle Catholic, I had no problem accepting Mary and the Church's teaching on her. I believed that she was conceived without original sin and was the mother of Jesus and that we could turn to her in prayer. There was also no doubt in my mind that she was very important to those of us who were Catholic. But in all honesty, I just didn't get why I needed her. Again, if I was going to pray, I wasn't going to waste time speaking to a fellow creature. I would go right to the top and speak to the Lord!

As my faith grew, however, the thought of Mary kept entering my mind. I wondered why so many holy people were devoted to her. Realizing that I must be missing something, I made it a priority to learn more about the Blessed Mother. Specifically, I wanted to discover how she could help me grow closer to Jesus.

### To Jesus through Mary

In the summer of 2011, I attended the Catholic Marketing Network trade show in the Philadelphia area. Even though I was still working full time as a project manager, I had been doing some Catholic radio and blogging on the side. I kept getting the idea that I should be doing full-time ministry, so I had made the decision to take a vacation day and do some networking at the trade show.

As I walked up and down the aisles handing out business cards and introducing myself, I ran into a gentleman named Ray Mooney who was there to promote a devotion called Total Consecration to Jesus through Mary. Ray's sincerity and dedication made me pause and listen to what he had to say. As he explained how Mary can bring us closer to Jesus, I realized that this could be the answer to my search: Perhaps I could finally understand Mary's role in my life. Ray gave me some literature and explained how I could consecrate my life to Jesus through Mary using the method popularized by St. Louis de Montfort.

Even as I turned my attention back to my main goal of networking, Ray's words kept echoing in my head. Later, after reading through the literature, I was interested but still a bit hesitant. I liked the overall concept (giving your life to Mary and letting her lead you to Jesus), but I wasn't sold. What if this devotion wasn't legitimate? What if it ended up taking me away from Jesus?

I went to the website run by Ray Mooney's organization (www.MyConsecration.org) and learned just how legitimate this devotion was. Endorsements by several popes and the fact that St. Louis de Montfort was a canonized saint took away any fears about its validity. However, I still wasn't sure that it was right for me. Not wanting to write it off, I decided to read St. Louis de Montfort's *True Devotion to Mary*. Upon opening the book, I read this message on the first page:

> The more we honor the Blessed Virgin, the more we honor Jesus Christ, because we honor Mary only that we may the more perfectly honor Jesus, since we go to her only as the way by which we are to find the end we are seeking, which is Jesus.[12]

Although I still didn't understand how it worked, I liked the overall objective: honoring Jesus Christ! As I read through the book, my fears began to fade away, and I felt increasingly drawn to consecrate my life to Jesus through Mary. What changed my mind?

For the most part, I realized that I wasn't as close to Jesus as I should be. I definitely needed to know him better. Once I understood that the purpose of Total Consecration was to draw me closer to Christ and help me better live out my baptismal promises, I knew that I had to act on it. If the Church gives me a way to grow closer to Jesus and I say, "No, thanks," how important is the goal to me? Combined with the fact that I wanted to get to know Mary, the decision really was a no-brainer.

Once I made the decision, I was so excited about Total Consecration that I promoted it on my nightly radio show. I invited listeners to join me for the thirty-three-day preparation period, followed by the consecration itself. Since it's recommended that the consecration be made on a Marian feast day, I had searched for the next such day and determined that I would consecrate my life to Jesus through Mary on the memorial of Our Lady of the Rosary—October 7. So along with several hundred radio listeners, I began the preparation process on September 4, 2011.

As we went through the daily prayers and meditations, most of us weren't sure what to expect. One thing that I definitely didn't expect was to come down with a nasty case of shingles a few weeks into the preparation! I was determined to get through it, however, and I managed to read the prayers on the air despite having a rather disgusting swollen lip for several days.

When the big day arrived, I followed St. Louis's advice and formally consecrated my life to Jesus through Mary after daily Mass. Initially I was disappointed, because I didn't feel any different. As I have come to learn, however, basing spiritual growth on feelings is a big mistake. Even though I didn't feel anything, my life was about to change in a big way!

MARY'S HELP

Prior to making my Total Consecration, I was struggling greatly in my job as a project manager. Not only did I not enjoy what I did, but I wasn't especially good at it! For close to thirty years, I worked as a software developer, and now I was in a position where I had to manage tasks, people, and budgets. My dream job was to work full-time for the Lord, but I just didn't know how it would be possible.

I spent many stress-filled days at the office wishing I was somewhere else. No matter how hard I tried, I couldn't accept the notion that this was where I needed to be. On the other hand, I didn't have many alternatives, and I needed to provide for my family.

One day, I was taking the dog for a walk and saying some prayers when I felt moved to say something that I never thought I'd be able to say. As I rounded a corner (I still remember exactly where it occurred), I told the Lord that if he needed me to stay in my current job, then it was OK with me. Even though I was shocked by what I said, I felt very comfortable saying it. Immediately after uttering these words, I was filled with a strong sense of peace.

At that moment, for the first time in many years, I wanted what the Lord wanted. In my mind, there's no way I could have accepted this on my own. Someone was definitely helping me. I understood that this peace was the first noticeable fruit of my Total Consecration. As promised, Mary drew me closer to Jesus by helping me accept his will for my life.

This was a big deal for me, and some even bigger changes were in the works. A few months after I made my consecration, something incredible happened. It was an answer to my prayer and a frightening nightmare at the same time. I was laid off from my day job!

While my initial feeling was one of panic (this was the first time that I had ever lost a job), it didn't take very long for a feeling of peace and gratitude to set in. My job had been making me miserable and also physically ill. Getting laid off actually relieved much of my stress and gave me the opportunity to work for the Lord on a full-time basis. I was ready to embark on an exciting new adventure, working for the greatest boss imaginable!

As the months (and years) passed, I never regretted consecrating my life to Jesus through Mary. In fact, I have renewed my consecration each fall, and I continue to lead listeners through the process on my Internet radio show. To date, I have led over two thousand individuals through the thirty-three-day preparation period and hope to continue to lead others through it. I have grown much closer not only to Mary but to Jesus. I have a greater desire to spend time with him in prayer, Eucharistic Adoration, reading the Bible, and daily Mass. Just as promised by St. Louis de Montfort, Mary has indeed brought me (and continues to bring me) closer to Jesus.

How Does It Work?
What is it about Marian devotion that causes us to grow closer to Jesus?

The beautiful thing about the way Mary operates is that we don't have to fully understand her involvement for it to be effective. Too many times we feel we need to completely understand how various devotions work in order for them to be fruitful. Not true. Mary's intercession doesn't work because we understand it; it works because we turn to her and she helps us!

But in case you'd like to have a better idea of how Our Lady operates, the wedding at Cana (John 2:1–11) is a good place to start. Mary (along with Jesus and his disciples) attended a wedding in the town of Cana in Galilee. We are told that a potential disaster occurred at the wedding: The wine ran out! As you can probably imagine, this was not a good thing. Wedding celebrations back in the time of Jesus could last a week or two, and a shortage of wine would reflect poorly on the bride and groom.

When the wine failed, Mary stepped into action. But she didn't try to fix the problem by herself. Instead, she went to Jesus and informed him of what had happened. This is the only time in the Bible when Mary approached Jesus on behalf of someone else. And how did it turn out? Jesus performed a miracle (his first) and saved the day.

Did Jesus really need Mary to tell him that the wine had run out? No. He knows all things. What possible reason could he have for letting his mother bring the problem to his attention? How about if he wanted us to turn to her when we're in trouble? Makes sense, doesn't it? The Bible, the inspired Word of God, gives us a powerful message here: The Lord is clearly showing us how Mary leads us to him.

As you read this story (and I recommend you do), take note of the role of the bride and groom. They are barely mentioned. They had a problem, however, and one of their guests (Jesus) had the power to solve it. They probably didn't know Jesus could restore the wine; this would be "the first of his signs" (John 2:11). Perhaps they didn't even know the wine had run out.

Whatever the case may be, Mary was the person who brought the problem to the attention of Jesus. She didn't tell him how to fix it; she just brought it to his attention, because she knew that he could handle it. In the same way, Mary will bring us to Jesus if we turn to her.

I would strongly recommend Total Consecration to anyone who desires to grow closer to Jesus. If you would like to learn more, you can visit www.MyConsecration.org or www. MontfortPublications.com. In addition, Fr. Michael Gaitley has written an excellent book on the subject, *33 Days to Morning Glory* (Marian, 2011), which will help you better understand the concept of Marian consecration.

## AT HOME WITH MARY

While formal consecration is a great thing, it's not the only way to grow close to Mary and allow her to bring you to Jesus. If you would like to see how Mary speaks to us through the Scriptures, I recommend my book *Listen to Your Blessed Mother* (Liguori, 2013). Another very good Marian book is *The Miraculous Medal: Stories, Prayers, and Devotions* by Donna-Marie Cooper O'Boyle (Servant, 2013).

Many saints have observed that the more we love the Blessed Mother, the more we will love Jesus. There are many ways that you can turn to Mary. The rosary, Pope St. John Paul told us, "remains… a prayer of great significance, destined to bring forth a harvest of holiness."[13] Fr. Michael Gaitley, in the appendices of his *33 Days to Morning Glory*, gives other prayers and devotions that can help us draw nearer to Our Lady. And speaking to Mary informally is another great way to let her lead you to Jesus.

Don't worry too much about how Mary works. Simply get to know her and allow her to help you. You will be amazed at what she will do.

As he was dying on the cross (and suffering terribly), Jesus summoned the strength to utter some very important words:

> When Jesus saw his mother, and the disciple whom he loved standing near, he said to his mother, "Woman, behold, your son!" Then he said to the disciple, "Behold, your mother!" And from that hour the disciple took her to his own home. (John 19:26–27)

Can you imagine how difficult it was for the Lord to speak at this time? What he had to say must have been very important—and it was. Speaking to his mother, Jesus gave her a son—the "disciple whom he loved" (commonly thought to be John). Then turning to the beloved disciple, he gave him the gift of a spiritual mother. We are told that the disciple accepted the Lord's gift and "took her to his own home."

As beloved disciples, Jesus's gift is meant for us as well. John accepted the gift of Mary on that day. How about you?

Don't Forget…

1. Mary exists to bring us to Jesus.
2. Growing closer to Mary will always draw us closer to Jesus.
3. Jesus performed his first miracle (changing the water into wine) at the request of his mother.
4. Total Consecration to Jesus through Mary is a formal, Church-approved way to let Mary help you grow closer to Jesus.
5. While dying on the cross, Jesus presented us with the gift of his own mother. It's up to us to accept that gift.

Jesus Says…

"Behold, your mother!" (John 19:27)

* « *

If any one says, "I love God," and hates his brother, he is a liar;
for he who does not love his brother whom he has seen, cannot
love God whom he has not seen.

—1 JOHN 4:20

No book on growing closer to Jesus would be complete
without making mention of the importance of seeing
him in others. I wanted to begin this section with a cute little
story that would gently lead into the importance of loving our
neighbor. After leaving Mass one day, I drove around asking the
Lord to give me a story. Specifically, I tried to think of something
that would emphasize the fact that how we treat our neighbor
(which includes our family members and even our enemies) is
how we treat Jesus.

Many things came to mind, such as the way I feel when
someone insults a member of my family or disrespects the
Catholic Church. Even though I might not be involved in the
incident, I take it very personally. If you hurt someone I love,
you hurt me.

As I mulled it over, however, none of these stories seemed
adequate. This step contains one of the most challenging

messages of the entire book and one that I don't want to sugar-coat. Therefore, I'm going to give it to you straight.

The way you treat other people is the way you treat Jesus. If you treat them with kindness and compassion, that's how you are treating the Lord. Period! If you treat them with contempt or ignore their needs, you got it—that's how you're treating him.

If we are serious about getting to know Jesus, there is no way that it will happen if we fail to see him in other people. As challenging as it is, this is absolutely necessary. Yet, it is something that many devout Christians seem to ignore.

## Jesus's Distressing Disguise

Why is this such a difficult concept to put into practice? As someone who struggles with this frequently, I see a few reasons.

First, the people in my life are not Jesus. They don't look like him (we all have our own image of what he looks like), they don't speak as he does, and they often don't act as he does. And there's a reason for this: They are not Jesus! Jesus Christ is the incarnate Word of God, "the image of the invisible God, the firstborn of all creation" (Colossians 1:15)! It's difficult for me to look at those around me and see Jesus in them.

Second, being nice to people can be challenging. It's not all that difficult when they are being nice to me, but it's a different story when they aren't very lovable. And in all honesty, nobody is lovable all of the time. We all have our moments.

On the other hand, it's not that tough to love Jesus, because he is all-loving. From the Gospels, he also appears quite vulnerable. When we think of how he was treated, we become sad. These feelings can be especially strong during Holy Week, when we recall how much he suffered. Our sadness grows when we make the connection that we were the cause of his suffering and death. As a result, at least for a few days, we make an effort to love Jesus more. We find time to pray, express sorrow for our sins, and follow his commandments. It's not all that difficult, because Jesus is very lovable, and we feel a certain sense of obligation.

Another reason it's easier to love Jesus than our neighbor is that we can ignore Jesus when his presence isn't convenient. When we have other things to deal with, we can close the Bible and forget about the Lord's instructions and needs. But it's not as easy to ignore a grouchy husband or the homeless person you encounter on the street. Jesus will let you forget about himself (at least temporarily), but it's another story with those individuals who cross our paths each day. Somehow, we have to deal with them.

Another challenge we face in treating everyone like Christ is that we can be very self-centered. I am often so focused on my own problems that I don't care about the problems of others. People dying of starvation can seem less important than the fact that my cable service isn't working. When it's a rainy and miserable day, praying for those who are suffering with cancer is not the first thing on my mind. If I'm not careful, my problems (even if they are relatively small) can become all that I think of.

This tendency to be self-centered can extend from not caring about the problems of others to not being overly concerned about the feelings of others. If we think that we've been treated poorly, our instinct is to stand up for our rights. While this isn't necessarily wrong, our emotions can sometimes cause us to lose control of the situation.

As someone who has fallen victim to this on many occasions, I know how easy it is to slip up. I find myself in the middle of an argument, not exactly sure how I let things get so out of control. It's not easy to treat someone like Christ while I'm in the process of yelling at the person!

So how do we handle this? How can we learn to remember that the way we treat those around us is the way we treat Christ?

## WISDOM FROM JESUS

One of the most effective ways I have found is to listen to the words of Jesus as he discusses what Judgment Day will be like. Every time I hear this Bible passage, I feel uncomfortable—and that's a good thing. There is nothing I could write that could make the message any clearer than what Jesus said toward the end of his public ministry:

> When the Son of man comes in his glory, and all the angels with him, then he will sit on his glorious throne. Before him will be gathered all the nations, and he will separate them one from another as a shepherd separates the sheep from the goats, and he will place the sheep at his right hand, but the goats at the left. (Matthew 25:31–33)

No problem so far. Most of us realize that we will be judged one day and that our actions will determine where we spend eternity. If we choose to follow the Lord, we will live with him forever in heaven. On the other hand, if we didn't want him in our life on earth, he will grant us our wish for eternity. We will be able to live without him forever—in hell.

Then the King will say to those at his right hand, "Come,

O blessed of my Father, inherit the kingdom prepared for you from the foundation of the world; for I was hungry and you gave me food, I was thirsty and you gave me drink, I was a stranger and you welcomed me, I was naked and you clothed me, I was sick and you visited me, I was in prison and you came to me." (Matthew 25:34–36)

This makes perfect sense. Jesus appears to be saying what most of us already know: If we treat him with love, we will be rewarded with eternal life in heaven. But Jesus hasn't yet dropped the bomb. What follows will raise the bar tremendously.

Then the righteous will answer him, "Lord, when did we see you hungry and feed you, or thirsty and give you drink? And when did we see you a stranger and welcome you, or naked and clothe you? And when did we see you sick or in prison and visit you?" And the King will answer them, "Truly, I say to you, as you did it to one of the least of these my brethren, you did it to me." (Matthew 25:37–40)

There are two ways we can react to the above Bible passage. We can ignore it, or we can take it seriously. As much as I'd like to soften the blow here, I can't. If we choose to ignore Jesus's words, we will spend eternity in hell. For Jesus goes on to say of those on his left, those who did not feed the hungry, clothe the naked, and so on, "They will go away into eternal punishment" (Matthew 25:46).

Please don't ignore the Lord's words. If you do, it will be the biggest mistake you'll ever make.

### OVERCOMING ANNOYANCE

While we're on the subject of mistakes, don't assume that writing a check to your favorite charity each month will fulfill the Lord's instructions. His message extends beyond that. Although it is necessary to share what we have with those in need, we are also required to love every person we meet. Yes, this includes those who might be seen as unlovable. It even includes our enemies. If we fail to do this, we are not only hurting our relationship with Jesus but jeopardizing our salvation.

Let's pause from the serious talk for a bit and discuss the good news. You and I can encounter Jesus in every person we meet today. That truly is a special privilege, don't you think? It also makes it much easier to be nice to people—provided we can get by the tendency to become annoyed by those we encounter. How do we overcome that very common tendency?

The first step is to read and reread Jesus's message in Matthew 25:31–46. His words are difficult to get around. We need to treat others with kindness.

If you're having trouble being kind to others, pray about it. Ask the Lord to help you. This is especially important when you find yourself in an encounter with a person who tries your patience. A quick, silent prayer (Help me, Lord!) has the potential to work miracles.

If you need additional help, I strongly recommend the book *The Hidden Power of Kindness* by Fr. Lawrence Lovasik. I have used this book on my radio show many times and have received tremendous feedback. It is one of the most helpful spiritual books I have ever read.

Being kind to those around us is one of the most overlooked

ways to grow closer to Christ, but it's also one of the most important. In order to put it into practice, we have to get over the fact that many of the people we meet don't remind us of Jesus. How can we clear that difficult hurdle? With God's help, all things are possible.

Don't make the mistake of trying to do it all by yourself. Follow the example of St. Paul: "Who is weak, and I am not weak?... I will all the more gladly boast of my weaknesses, that the power of Christ may rest upon me" (2 Corinthians 11:29; 12:9). Admit that you're weak, especially when it comes to seeing Jesus in those around you. Ask Jesus to help you, and he will.

Once you begin to recognize the Lord in everyone you meet, you are going to see much more of him every day. And that is always a positive development!

DON'T FORGET...
1. The way we treat other people is the way we treat Jesus.
2. Through those around us, we have the opportunity to encounter Christ several times each day.
3. If we expect to get to heaven, we must help those who are less fortunate.
4. Even though it's often difficult to see him, Jesus is present in everyone we meet.
5. If you are struggling to get along with a difficult person, don't forget to ask the Lord for help.

JESUS SAYS...
"Truly, I say to you, as you did it to one of the least of these my brethren, you did it to me." (Matthew 25:40)

* * *

Be strong and of good courage; be not frightened, neither be
dismayed; for the Lord your God is with you wherever you go.
—JOSHUA 1:9

As we go through our day dealing with responsibilities,
problems, and experiences, it's very easy to forget about
the Lord. The fact that we can't see him with our eyes and hear
him with our ears often makes us lose sight of the fact that he
is always with us. In order to have a quality relationship with
him, we have to come up with a way to overcome this problem.

Let's look at some relatively easy ways to live in the Lord's
presence throughout the day. These steps require some work,
but there's nothing here that you can't handle. With a little
effort, you'll become very aware of the presence of Christ no
matter where you go or what you're doing.

OUR UBIQUITOUS LORD
Before we get to the specifics, let's address one important point.
The Lord is always with us.

> Where shall I go from your Spirit?
>    Or where shall I flee from your presence?
> If I ascend to heaven, you are there!
>    If I make my bed in Sheol, you are there!

If I take the wings of the morning
　　and dwell in the uttermost parts of the sea,
even there your hand shall lead me,
　　and your right hand shall hold me. (Psalm 139:7–10)

The steps suggested in this step are not going to make Jesus show up in our lives. He's already there! These steps are designed to help us recognize his presence. It's a great gift to have Jesus with us wherever we go. Becoming more aware of him is definitely going to change the way we do business and bring us much peace.

If you think you're the only one who has trouble recognizing Jesus, you're wrong. The Bible records a few such occurrences. Before we explore some ways to become more aware of the Lord's presence, let's look at some individuals who had difficulty recognizing Jesus at certain points in time. Fortunately, they all ended up discovering him, and you can too.

## THE ROAD TO EMMAUS (LUKE 24:13–35)

This has always been one of my favorite biblical stories, and it is one that I speak about frequently in parishes. Two disciples (Cleopas and one who is unnamed) are journeying to a town named Emmaus. We are told that it is seven miles from Jerusalem, but scholars have never pinpointed its exact location. This fact is important, because it implies that (like so many of us), these two disciples were not sure where they were headed!

Jesus had already risen from the grave, and he joined these travelers on the journey. Unfortunately, they didn't recognize him. When the Lord asked them what they were discussing, they told the story of the crucifixion. They also expressed sadness because of the fact that they "had hoped that he was the one to redeem Israel" (Luke 24:21).

Jesus proceeded to show them the references to him in the Scriptures, but still they didn't recognize him. Then something happened: "When he was at table with them, he took the bread and blessed and broke it, and gave it to them. And their eyes were opened and they recognized him" (Luke 24:30–31).

Do the actions of Jesus remind you of anything? It sounds like what happens at Mass, doesn't it? One of the best ways to live in the presence of Christ is to make an effort to attend daily Mass. Even one or two days a week (in addition to Sunday) will make a big difference in your life.

### MARY MAGDALENE AT THE TOMB (JOHN 20:1–18)

Like the disciples traveling to Emmaus, Mary Magdalene underestimated the power of the Lord. She went to his tomb, saw that the stone had been removed, and assumed that his body had been taken. After alerting Peter and John to the apparent theft, she stood weeping outside of the tomb. She had no idea that a miracle had taken place.

In a sense, we're no different. We often fail to see the Lord working in the unpleasant circumstances of our life. The good news is that Jesus understands our blindness and will continually reach out to us and let us know that things aren't as bad as they seem. That's exactly what happened with Mary Magdalene. Just as he did with the pilgrims traveling to Emmaus, Jesus appeared to Mary.

Once again, Jesus was not recognized. Even after he spoke to her, Mary failed to identify him. Thinking that Jesus was the gardener, she pleaded: "Sir, if you have carried him away, tell me where you have laid him, and I will take him away" (John 20:15).

Jesus responded with one word—"Mary." That's all it took for her eyes to be opened. She was now able to recognize the presence of the Lord.

What happened here? One of the key things that Mary did was to seek the Lord. Even though she was confused and she misinterpreted what had happened, she continued to look for Jesus. Asking the man she thought was the gardener led to a response that clarified what was taking place.

When Christ called Mary by name, she knew that it was he. Do you believe that the Lord knows your name? Do you make the effort to hear him call you by name? Remember this Bible verse: "Fear not, for I have redeemed you; I have called you by name, you are mine" (Isaiah 43:1). That message is so powerful that you cannot hear it too many times.

### The Finding of Jesus in the Temple (Luke 2:41–52)

Considering the fact that the Blessed Mother was conceived without original sin and never committed a personal sin, one would expect that she wouldn't understand what it feels like to be separated from Jesus. This is one documented case, however, that shows she knew exactly what it felt like.

After traveling to Jerusalem with Jesus for Passover, Mary and Joseph departed for home, leaving the Lord behind. And to make things worse, they traveled for an entire day before realizing it!

Now, lest you assume that Mary and Joseph were irresponsible, it's important to point out that it was a common practice for the men and women to travel in separate caravans.

Therefore, it's entirely possible that Mary thought that Jesus was with Joseph and vice versa. Eventually, the couple realized that they had become separated from the Lord.

Let's pause for a minute and think about our own lives. How many times each day, whether by sin or by distraction, do we find ourselves in the position of being separated from Jesus? It happens to me all the time, and that is why I'm including this section in the book. Mary and Joseph will do something to remedy the situation. We can learn an important lesson from them.

Once they realized that Jesus was missing, Mary and Joseph "returned to Jerusalem, seeking him" (Luke 2:45). Their efforts were rewarded, and after three days, they found him sitting in the Temple.

While this is a familiar story, one of the most important details often goes overlooked. Confused as to why Jesus had remained in the Temple (remember that Mary was human and sometimes unclear as to why things happened), Mary addressed her Son with the following words: "Son, why have you treated us so? Behold, your father and I have been looking for you anxiously" (Luke 2:48).

In addition to the obvious sadness that Mary and Joseph experienced (which is apparent when looking at the Greek manuscript of this verse), there is a sense of urgency implied. They needed to get Jesus back in their lives. How anxious are you to do the same thing? Is being in the Lord's presence throughout the day a priority for you?

I have a hunch that you do care, and I recommend that you pray for the grace to care even more. After all, you're going to work harder at something that is important to you. If living in the presence of the Lord really matters to you, you'll do what's necessary to make it happen. With that in mind, let's explore some simple ways to become aware of the Lord's presence every day.

### Day-by-Day with Jesus

As soon as you wake up in the morning, thank the Lord for giving you another day. Spend a few minutes thinking about the fact that he is almighty and has created everything (including you) out of nothing. Ask Jesus to help you see him in every situation. Remember, you don't want to manage your life on your own; that would be a mistake. With all of the distractions we face each day, we need the Lord's help so that we can see him in all that happens and in everyone we meet. So ask him to help you.

Going back to step 3, commit yourself to daily prayer. This will make a healthy relationship with Jesus grow. It follows that you will become more and more aware of his presence throughout the day.

Visit Jesus in the Blessed Sacrament. We discussed this in step 6, but it definitely bears repeating. Stopping by the Adoration chapel or church for even five minutes can be incredibly helpful. If at all possible, receive Jesus at daily Mass. It will definitely change your life.

Use visual aids. When I worked in an office, I always had several pictures of Eileen and the girls on my desk. This made it feel as if they were with me. It also reminded me of the reason that I was working for a living—to provide for them. In the same way, holy cards and pictures of the Lord serve as reminders of his constant presence. Placing these images in strategic places (around your computer, near your phone, on a mirror) will help you remember that Jesus is always with you, to treat others with kindness, and to avoid impure thoughts or actions.

Listen to Christian music. I have always been a big fan of music; without a doubt, it can alter my mood. Listening to sad songs makes me feel sad, and listening to positive songs generally makes me feel happy. It only makes sense that listening to songs about the Lord will make us think about him and his message—whether it's contemporary Christian, Gregorian chant, Gospel, or hymns.

Call your spiritual mother each day and ask for help. As we discussed in step 7, Mary's main function is to bring us closer to Jesus. She did this in a big way two thousand years ago, and she continues to do it today. Call on her each day, and ask her to help you grow closer to Jesus. You will not be disappointed!

Do something kind for someone. This is not the first thing we think of when trying to live in the presence of the Lord, but it's one of the most effective ways to make it happen. Every day, multiple people cross our paths, many of whom we will never meet again. Each of these encounters provides an opportunity to meet Jesus. Can you make it a point to perform at least one unselfish act each day? You'll be amazed at how much closer you'll come to Christ.

As you go through the day, make it a point to reach out to the Lord and ask for the grace to deal with the situations you encounter. Before going to sleep, spend a few minutes examining your conscience. Think back on the events of the day. If you feel you handled things incorrectly, tell Jesus you're sorry and ask for the grace to do better the next day. For those situations you handled well, thank him for the grace that enabled you to do so. Finally, ask him to protect you and your loved ones as you sleep.

You don't have to do each of these things every day in order to grow in your awareness of Jesus's presence. I recommend that you try them all and see which ones work best for you. Some may seem unnatural at first; putting them into practice will grow easier with time. Those that are right for you will eventually become habits. Then you'll really start to see progress.

No matter where you go or what you do, Jesus is with you. The challenge is to see him. If you make the effort, you'll see him wherever you go.

DON'T FORGET...

1. Although we sometimes lose sight of him, Jesus is always with us.
2. If we seek the Lord throughout the day, we will find him.
3. Taking steps to become aware of Jesus's presence requires work at first, but it will become much easier as time goes on.
4. When trying to remain aware of the Lord's presence, it's very important that we make use of our senses.
5. Don't forget to ask Mary to help you become more aware of her Son's presence in your life.

JESUS SAYS...

"I am with you always, to the close of the age." (Matthew 28:20)

## step ten Don't Waste Your Suffering

❋ ❋ ❋

The Lord is near to the brokenhearted,
and saves the crushed in spirit.
—PSALM 34:18

Before we discuss the tenth way to become closer friends with Jesus, I want to deliver some good news about it. Although the previous nine steps are amazingly easy, they require you to actively do something. If you don't seek, you won't find. In order for you to serve the poor, read the Bible, visit Jesus in the Blessed Sacrament, learn and obey the teachings of the Church, and follow all the other recommendations, some degree of activity on your part is required. The burden is relatively light, but it does rest on your shoulders.

This final step is different in that the Lord is the one who takes the active role and makes it happen. Your job is simply to respond to what he sends.

Suffering is a part of everyone's life. Even those who don't have a relationship with the Lord will experience suffering. We don't have to look for suffering. Every day we are presented with some form of it. It often gets overlooked because it's relatively minor (headaches, traffic jams, tiredness, bad weather, boredom), but it's there. At other times the suffering is all we can think about because it is overwhelming—suffering such as sudden death, serious illness, severe pain, and financial disaster.

Big or little, suffering is suffering. Because of its unpleasant nature, we typically think of it as a bad thing. However, suffering can be beneficial in that it can draw us closer to Jesus.

THE GIFT OF PAIN

In his Letter to the Romans, St. Paul teaches us "that in everything God works for good with those who love him, who are called according to his purpose" (Romans 8:28). Everything that happens in our lives can help us get to heaven, even if it involves suffering. This is one of the most powerful messages in the Bible and one that I mention in almost every talk that I give. Paul's words remind us that, in his almighty power, God can bring good out of anything—including tragedy and devastation. There is no better example of this than the crucifixion of Jesus Christ. The most horrific crime imaginable resulted in our redemption.

While no suffering could ever compare with the torture and murder of the Son of God, tragic and seemingly senseless things do happen. We hear daily of the deaths of innocent children, acts of terror, and natural disasters that wipe out innocent lives. Suffering hits our own lives—perhaps even "tribulation, or distress, or persecution, or famine, or nakedness, or peril, or sword" (Romans 8:35). Romans 8:28 reminds us that the Lord always has a plan. In the end, suffering can help us grow closer to the Lord and help us get to heaven.

How can suffering draw us closer to Christ? In his apostolic letter *Salvifici Doloris* (On the Christian Meaning of Human Suffering), Pope St. John Paul II provides some great insight:

Down through the centuries and generations it has been seen that *in suffering there is concealed* a particular *power that draws a person interiorly close to Christ*, a special grace. To this grace many saints, such as Saint Francis of Assisi, Saint Ignatius of Loyola and others, owe their profound conversion. A result of such a conversion is not only that the individual discovers the salvific meaning of suffering but above all that he becomes a completely new person. He discovers a new dimension, as it were, of *his entire life and vocation*. This discovery is a particular confirmation of the spiritual greatness which in man surpasses the body in a way that is completely beyond compare. When this body is gravely ill, totally incapacitated, and the person is almost incapable of living and acting, all the more do interior *maturity and spiritual greatness* become evident, constituting a touching lesson to those who are healthy and normal. (*Salvifici Doloris*, 26)[14]

Even if we know that suffering can be a good thing and can bring us closer to Christ, however, it's still a bitter pill to swallow. Human beings don't like to suffer and have a tendency to avoid it at all costs. Is there anything we can do to change that?

Let's start with a powerful statement from St. Paul. Remarkably, it's something he wrote while he was in prison: "Now I rejoice in my sufferings for your sake, and in my flesh I complete what is lacking in Christ's afflictions for the sake of his body, that is, the Church" (Colossians 1:24).

For most of us, the idea of rejoicing over suffering is incomprehensible. Paul was not alone in his belief, however. St. Thérèse of Lisieux expressed the same opinion: "Is there any greater joy than to suffer for love of You?"[15] These saints do not enjoy pain and agony, but they understand its value in God's plan of salvation.

Suffering allows us the opportunity to climb on the cross with Jesus and participate in his redemptive mission. Think about that for a minute. By enduring the suffering that comes into our lives, we share in the mission of Jesus. This is made possible because of the fact that we are part of his Mystical Body (the Church) and therefore can participate in his sacrifice on the cross. He did his part, and now we have the opportunity to do our part.

How important of a role do you play in the Mystical Body of Christ? Picture a symphony orchestra. Each musician works with the others to produce a beautiful symphony. If one plays the wrong part or is absent, the end result will suffer. Even though we, the audience, typically focus on the final product, the role of each musician is critical. Without everyone playing his or her part, there would be no symphony.

At the same time, no one musician operates in a vacuum. All have sheet music to guide them, and they must follow the directions of the conductor. If each of them shows up, takes the assigned seat, follows the sheet music, and pays attention to the conductor's instructions, beautiful music will result.

Every day, you and I have a reserved seat as part of Christ's orchestra, his Mystical Body. If we don't willingly occupy our seats and perform our roles, something will be missing. Nobody else can perform your particular role. What is your role? As a Christian, you are asked to follow Jesus—wherever he goes.

By accepting the suffering that comes into your life, you are following him to a very important place—to the cross on Calvary.

### A Look at Jesus's Passion

Knowing that our suffering can unite us more closely with Jesus isn't enough to make us thrilled about embracing it. The first thing that comes to mind might be, "He can handle it, but I can't." Depending on how severe the pain is, we sometimes can think of nothing besides trying to make it disappear. Willingly embracing our cross is often the last thing on our minds. If the problem doesn't go away, it often seems more natural to complain.

I personally feel that one of the best ways to combat this very common feeling is to take a closer look at the suffering that Jesus endured for us. By doing so, we'll be more willing to help him by patiently accepting the difficulties that we encounter. Where should we begin? Let's look at the sorrowful mysteries of the rosary and briefly discuss how each applies to our lives.

• *The Agony in the Garden*

> And he withdrew from them about a stone's throw, and knelt down and prayed, "Father, if you are willing, remove this chalice from me; nevertheless not my will, but yours, be done." And there appeared to him an angel from heaven, strengthening him. And being in an agony he prayed more earnestly; and his sweat became like great drops of blood falling down upon the ground. (Luke 22:41–44)

Make no mistake about it; Jesus knew what it was like to suffer. On the night before he died, the Lord taught us a great lesson. When we suffer, it's perfectly acceptable to pray that the suffering will end. Jesus asked for the chalice of suffering to be removed. We should feel free to do that also.

Sometimes the Lord will choose to allow our suffering to continue. If that is the case, he will give us the grace to persevere. Jesus accepted the Father's answer, and he was given an angel to strengthen him. We should say yes to God and expect his aid.

- *The Scourging at the Pillar*

    Then Pilate took Jesus and scourged him. (John 19:1)

Matthew, Mark, and John all mention the scourging of Jesus, but they tell us little about the process. Scourging was a brutal punishment inflicted on Roman prisoners prior to their execution. It involved being tied to a stone post and repeatedly whipped on the back with cords tipped with iron balls. The process would render victims close to death. Jesus voluntarily subjected himself to this agony out of love for us. He willingly suffered this so that we could be redeemed.

How are you being scourged today? Do you have a chronic illness? Are you finding it difficult to deal with a certain person? Have you asked the Lord to remove the problem, but it still remains? Until the problem goes away, are you willing to endure your scourging out of love for Jesus? If so, you will be imitating him by willingly suffering for him just as he suffered for you.

- *The Crowning with Thorns*

    And they stripped him and put a scarlet robe upon him, and plaiting a crown of thorns they put it on his head, and put a reed in his right hand. (Matthew 27:28–29)

We have a rosebush in back of our house, and I'm always amazed at the pain when I accidentally touch one of its thorns. It's hard to imagine how much it hurt Jesus to be forced to wear an entire crown made of thorns. That pain was probably enough to make most of us do whatever we could to escape the suffering. Not Jesus. He had a job to do, and he willingly submitted to every form of torture that was directed his way. In addition to the physical pain, he was also subject to the emotional pain of being spat upon and ridiculed.

This world is not perfect. There are many unpleasant things that you and I must face every day. Are you able to offer up the thorns that you encounter and remain focused on the bigger picture, or do you allow yourself to become frustrated when any kind of discomfort hits? That is the challenge.

The message of the world is to seek pleasure and avoid pain at all costs. The message of Christ is different. As Christians, we are pilgrims on a journey. We are traveling to our real home in heaven, and we need to travel through the cross. Keeping that in mind makes the suffering of daily life much easier to bear.

• *The Carrying of the Cross*
> So they took Jesus, and he went out, bearing his own cross,
> to the place called the place of a skull, which is called in
> Hebrew Golgotha. (John 19:17)

After being scourged and crowned with thorns, Jesus was then forced to carry his own cross to Calvary. Even though he was assisted by Simon of Cyrene (see Matthew 27:32; Mark 15:21; Luke 23:26), it was not easy for the weakened Jesus to exert himself in this manner. Although he could have taken care of the matter in any number of ways, the Lord once again chose to follow his Father's plan. This difficult journey was necessary for our redemption.

We all have crosses to carry. Some of them are very heavy. Do we embrace them, or do we complain and reject them?

As striking as it is to look at an image of the crucified Christ, there was a great deal of pain and agony that he endured even before getting to Calvary. It's important to remember that Jesus could have walked away from his sufferings at any time. But he loved us too much to do that. His pain was necessary for our salvation.

Are you willing to walk with Jesus as he carries his cross? By accepting the unavoidable suffering that comes your way, you are replying with a resounding yes.

- *The Crucifixion*

    And when they came to the place which is called The Skull, there they crucified him, and the criminals, one on the right and one on the left. (Luke 23:33)

After reading the previous meditations, I'm sure you realize that Christ's suffering wasn't limited to three hours on the cross. Nonetheless, this is where the ultimate sacrifice took place. It was on the cross that he gave all he had for our sake. Are you willing to give up your life for him?

Ultimately, we have to make a decision. If we truly want to be followers of Jesus, we must be willing to follow him everywhere. He won't force us to do it; it's something that you and I must do willingly. If we choose to play it safe and not follow him all the way, there will be eternal repercussions. "For whoever would save his life will lose it; and whoever loses his life for my sake, he will save it" (Luke 9:24).

When taken at face value, suffering is painful. On the other hand, uniting our sufferings with the Lord's can bring great peace and will eventually lead to eternal life in heaven. St. Faustina Kowalska tells of a powerful vision that she experienced. It reminds us of just how important it is to carry our crosses willingly.

> Then I saw the Lord Jesus nailed to the cross. When He had hung on it for a while, I saw a multitude of souls crucified like Him. Then I saw a second multitude of souls, and a third. The second multitude were not nailed to [their] crosses, but were holding them firmly in their hands. The third were neither nailed to [their] crosses nor holding them firmly in their hands, but were dragging [their] crosses behind them and were discontent. Jesus then said to me, Do you see these souls? Those who are like Me in the pain and contempt they suffer will be like Me also in glory. And those who resemble Me less in pain and contempt will also bear less resemblance to Me in glory.[16]

When we suffer, we have the opportunity to grow even closer to Jesus. Don't waste the chance. The momentary pain will bear eternal fruit.

DON'T FORGET...
1. Suffering gives us an opportunity to grow very close to Jesus.
2. As members of the Mystical Body of Christ, the Church, we are able to unite our sufferings with that of Jesus. By doing so, we can assist him with his redemptive mission.
3. Whether it's minor or major, we all experience some form of suffering each day.

4. If we remain close to Christ, we can experience peace even in the midst of great suffering.

5. Jesus willingly gave up his life for us. By accepting our crosses and following him (through good and bad times), we have the chance to give up our lives for him.

JESUS SAYS...

"If any man would come after me, let him deny himself and take up his cross daily and follow me." (Luke 9:23)

How about some good news? If you regularly practice the ten steps discussed in this book, you will become closer friends with Jesus Christ. Not may, not probably, but you will! The only thing that can prevent it from happening is if you give up.

I can make this bold claim because I know how the Lord operates. As the saying goes, he will not be outdone in generosity. If you put in the effort and spend time with him, he will reciprocate to a greater degree than you could imagine.

As promised, none of the steps are burdensome. Friendship with Jesus doesn't require advanced intelligence (look at the apostles!), great wealth, unlimited free time, or travel to exotic locations. Jesus Christ wants to be your friend. In order to become close friends with the Lord, all you have to do is try your best and let him do the rest.

For years I would go to Mass and not realize that I could become friends with Jesus. Maybe I thought it possible in a figurative sense, but not in a literal sense. I struggled through life and was miserable. I worried constantly and didn't think I could ever be peaceful. There were many occasions when my outlook bordered on hopelessness. I bought into the world's theory that happiness could only result from money, possessions, and the absence of problems. Sure, I had my happy times, but something would always come along and take away my happiness. That's what happens when you put your trust in worldly things.

Now that I have become friends with Jesus, I am experiencing peace as never before. While I still experience discouragement from time to time, it doesn't last. The minute I begin to experience negative thoughts or feel anxious, I run to the Lord. I love to imitate the beloved disciple and lie "close to the breast of Jesus" (John 13:23). Whether I'm conversing with him in prayer, listening to him speak through Scripture, or sitting in his presence at the adoration chapel, I feel secure. Any potential storms in my life fade away.

We all desire that kind of peace, and the Lord wants us to have it. The secret is to remain close to him.

Sadly, the world is filled with people who don't have a personal relationship with the Lord. As you would expect, they are lacking peace. Sleepwalking through their daily lives, they desperately seek happiness in the things of the world. When the temporary pleasures wear off, they are often plunged into despair.

Many of these people could be sitting next to you at Mass on Sunday. I know because I was in that place for many years. Just because someone goes to church doesn't mean that he or she knows Jesus on a personal level. You and I are called to change that.

Many people have either never heard of Jesus or don't believe that he is real. If we don't tell them, it's possible that no one will. This is not just a modern problem. St. Paul addressed it two thousand years ago: "But how are men to call upon him in whom they have not believed? And how are they to believe in him of whom they have never heard? And how are they to hear without a preacher?" (Romans 10:14). Once we discover Jesus, it's up to us to share him with others.

I used to think that evangelization was only for Protestants. The job of a Catholic, I thought, was to attend Mass on Sunday and abstain from eating meat on Lenten Fridays. Speaking about the Lord outside of Church wasn't something we did. Whenever I mention this in one of my talks, I see many heads begin to nod. I'm not sure what caused so many Catholics to feel this way, but it's definitely a common way of thinking. It's also very wrong.

The Church has always taught that evangelization is necessary. Jesus commands us, "Go...and make disciples of all nations" (Matthew 28:19). Pope Paul VI told the Church on the Feast of the Immaculate Conception back in 1975:

> Finally, the person who has been evangelized goes on to evangelize others. Here lies the test of truth, the touchstone of evangelization: it is unthinkable that a person should accept the Word and give himself to the kingdom without becoming a person who bears witness to it and proclaims it in his turn.[17]

Furthermore, sharing the Good News of Jesus Christ isn't just for the clergy and religious. Every layperson "who has been evangelized" is called to do it as well. Pope St. John Paul II made this point repeatedly:

> Recent popes have stressed the importance of the role of the laity in missionary activity. In the Exhortation *Christifideles Laici*, I spoke explicitly of the Church's

> "permanent mission of bringing the Gospel to the multi-
> tudes—the millions and millions of men and women—who
> as yet do not know Christ the Redeemer of humanity,"
> and of the responsibility of the lay faithful in this regard.
> The mission *ad gentes* is incumbent upon the entire People
> of God. Whereas the foundation of a new church requires
> the Eucharist and hence the priestly ministry, missionary
> activity, which is carried out in a wide variety of ways, is
> the task of all the Christian faithful.[18]

It is our job to share Jesus with those we encounter—by our
actions and with our words. We also should not be afraid to
present the whole truth. Jesus founded a Church and continues
to speak through that Church. As important as it is to have
a personal relationship with the Lord, that relationship needs
to be rooted in Catholic teaching. Separating Jesus from his
Church is a huge mistake. As we discussed in step 2, Christ and
his Church are inseparable.

The world can be a dark place; it is very much in need of the
Lord's message. As Christians, we have the secret to overcoming
the darkness, and his name is Jesus. I pray that you will not only
become close friends with him but also share him with those
around you. He is "the way, and the truth, and the life" (John
14:6). People need to hear about him.

Jesus is also the best friend you will ever have. It's an incredible privilege to know him. While there is no doubt that you
will experience trials in this life, you will never have to face
them alone. By your side will be the one who has overcome the
world. As expressed so perfectly by the Holy Spirit in the pages
of the Bible:

Even though I walk through the valley
  of the shadow of death,
  I fear no evil;
for you are with me;
  your rod and your staff,
  they comfort me. (Psalm 23:4)

CHAPTER THREE

1. *Miserentissimus Redemptor*, 13.

2. Jesus to St. Margaret Mary Alacoque, in *The Autobiography of St. Margaret Mary Alacoque*, trans. Sisters of the Visitation (Charlotte, N.C.: Tan, 2012), 56.

CHAPTER FOUR

3. Fulton J. Sheen, *Life of Christ* (New York: Doubleday, 2008), 42.

CHAPTER FIVE

4. *Dei Verbum*, 25, quoting St. Ambrose, *On the Duties of Ministers* I, 20, 88: PL l6, 50.

5. *Evangelii Gaudium*, 3. Pope Francis quotes Pope Paul VI, Apostolic Exhortation *Gaudete in Domino*, May 9, 1975, 22.

STEP TWO

6. *Catechism of the Catholic Church*, 2nd ed., is available at Catholic bookstores. You can also order it and view it online at the United States Conference of Catholic Bishops website, www.USCCB.org.

STEP THREE

7. St. Thérèse of Lisieux, *The Story of a Soul*, trans. John Beevers (New York: Doubleday, 2001), 118.

STEP FIVE

8. Pope Francis, as quoted in Domenico Agasso, Jr., "Francis: 'Pray with your heart, not like a parrot,'" *Vatican Insider*, May 16, 2014.

9. *Catechesi Tradendae*, 19.

STEP SIX

10. *Ecclesia de Eucharistia*, 25. The "art of prayer" is a reference to his apostolic letter *Novo Millennio Ineunte*.

11. Archbishop Fulton Sheen, *Treasure in Clay: The Autobiography of Fulton J. Sheen* (Garden City, N.Y.: Doubleday, 1980), 188–189, 190.

STEP SEVEN

12. St. Louis de Montfort, *True Devotion to Mary*, trans. Frederick William Faber (Rockford, Ill.: Tan, 1985), front matter.

13. St. John Paul II, *Rosarium Virginis Mariae*, 1.

STEP TEN

14. *Salvifici Doloris*, 26.

15. St. Thérèse, 118.

16. St. Faustina Kowalska, *Diary: Divine Mercy in My Soul* (Stockbridge, Mass.: Marians of the Immaculate Conception, 2003), 197.

CONCLUSION

17. *Evangelii Nuntiandi*, 24.

18. *Redemptoris Missio*, 71.

## About the Author

Gary Zimak is a full-time Catholic evangelist and author. He is a frequent speaker at parishes and conferences across the country and is widely known for his talks on overcoming anxiety. Gary hosts a daily radio show on BlogTalkRadio and is a regular guest on *Catholic Answers Live*, EWTN's *Son Rise Morning Show*, and *Catholic Connection with Teresa Tomeo*. A member of Catholics United for the Faith, the Knights of Columbus, and the Catholic Radio Association, he is an RCIA instructor at Sacred Heart Parish in Riverton, New Jersey, and the chaplain for the Catholic Business Network of South Jersey. Gary resides in New Jersey with his wife, Eileen, and twin daughters, Mary and Elizabeth.